D1566383

MYSTERIES OF THE HOLY GRAIL

MYSTERIES

OF THE

HOLY GRAIL

By

CORINNE HELINE

☆   ☆   ☆

NEW AGE BIBLE & PHILOSOPHY CENTER
1139 Lincoln Blvd.
Santa Monica, CA 90403

Grateful acknowledgement is hereby extended to Ann Barkhurst for her invaluable assistance in the preparation of this volume.

REPRINTED 1986

TABLE OF CONTENTS

PART V

CONCLUSION

THE TEMPLE

PART I

BACKGROUND

ARCHEOLOGY AND THE GRAIL

At Glastonbury, near the base of the two hills known as Chalice Hill and Glastonbury Tor, there is a sacred well, described variously in the Grail stories. This is the Chalice Well, into which the Chalice was, according to one story, dropped for safekeeping for a time. This reminds us of the modern discovery of the church lying under the cistern which is thought to be Christ's tomb, near Mount Golgotha. This ancient sanctuary and tomb had been hidden under the waters of the cistern for many centuries, until a leakage caused the water to drain away, and the ancient site was revealed. The tomb had evidently been the nucleus of a church where the Christians worshipped in secret.

We find also that when the Copper Scroll discovered in the Dead Sea Caves was finally deciphered, this proved to be a map and listing of hiding places of treasure, which had belonged perhaps to the Temple, or perhaps to the Essenes to be used when the Messiah returned; a number of these hiding places were cisterns. Legend has long had it that treasure belonging to the House of David had been hidden away, pending the Messiah's return; and it may well be that some of this treasure belonged not merely to the Temple bank, nor yet to the Messianic movement of Jesus' time, but was actually the property of the Kings of Judah in exile.

The Chalice Well is an ancient sacred fountain, pre-Christian in origin; and it is said that its waters are radioactive. So also the area in Bohemia associated in some legends with the Brothers of the Rose Cross is characterized by radioactive mountains. Mythologists are agreed that it is the Sacred Well which gave rise to the story of the Holy Grail or Druidic "Cauldron" with its bubbling waters.

In the twentieth century we have seen excitement in religious circles by the discovery of certain cups which it is thought might have been the true Cup of the Last Supper and hence the Grail of legend. One, a cup of Syrian blue grass, with Greek inscriptions upon it, was discovered in the museum at Toledo, Spain. The inscriptions read: "Be of good cheer," and "What are you here for?" (In the New Testament, Christ's words to Judas, "Friend, wherefore art thou come?") There are five such cups in existence which supports the tradition that six cups were used at the Last Supper. Two are in the Berlin Museum, one at Leyden, one in the British Museum, and one in Italy. The Toledo Cup is thought to be a copy of the so-called Antioch Cup, which is at present in the Metropolitan Museum in New York, and has been on display in the Cloisters there at various times. This chalice is a plain silver cup of common design which was found in the ruins of Antioch in 1910 and sent to the United States at the outbreak of the First World War. After nine years of research, Dr. Gustavus Eisen, an eminent scholar, produced a book, published in two large volumes under the title *The Great Chalice of Antioch,* in which he adduced evidence which he thought showed that this cup might well be the actual cup of the Last Supper. The cup itself is plain, but it is set in an elaborately worked silver dressing on which are inscribed representations of Christ and the Apostles who sat with Him at the Last Supper. The likenesses correspond with the traditional word descriptions found in ancient documents of the primitive Church.

It is said that this cup was kept at Glastonbury until the time of the Crusades, when it was entrusted to the Crusaders, and was lost in battle at Antioch and discovered there in 1910 by Arab excavators.

In some apocryphal accounts we read of a golden cup as being "the Cup of Prophecy," symbolizing the Secret Doctrine of Moses, handed down to the Seventy Elders of Israel on Mount Sinai. Again, the Serpent and Eagle are associated with the Gospel of John, and we are reminded of glyphs and pictures in which a Cup holds a serpent with upraised head, which, in one instance, St. John blesses.

The antiquity of this symbol is suggested in the Persian account of "the Cup of Jemshyd," the celestial "seven-ringed Cup" from which the legendary King quaffed wisdom.

Chapter I

AN INTERPRETATION OF GRAIL ORIGINS

Ageless wisdom, the first religion given to the early patriarchs by the angelic messengers of the gods, was transmitted whole from the spiritual world to early leaders of mankind. These Wise Ones, masters of other days, were men above creed and class. They served not idols but ideals. Theologies and philosophies grew up around them, yet each divine leader was greater than the Order which he founded. Melchizedek of biblical fame was one of these, King Arthur was another. From the same place they all came forth.

In man's first ages certain divinely instituted Mysteries were the intermediaries between man and the gods. These august institutions were the custodians of a superior learning by which the mind was inclined to a way of larger truth and deeper understanding. As mankind turned increasingly toward materialism, these sacred schools became corrupt. This is admirably portrayed in the coming and the passing of King Arthur.

The Holy Grail is a subject of perpetual and absorbing interest to the scholar, the artist and the occultist—through each of these approaches the study from a somewhat different point of view. Popular Christianity has, it is true, lost the enthusiasm for the Grail stories which was so conspicuous a feature of the nineteenth century in England and on the continent of Europe, perhaps because contemporary science has produced miracles which seem to overshadow the miracles of religion; but when the beautiful old tales are interpreted in the light of soul-illumination and Initiation into great Mysteries, the interest springs up anew as vital as it ever was. Perhaps these old legends were in need of a "rest," in need of a time of quiet in which to send their roots deeper into the mystic past of Christendom, whence also they first arose.

Although the legendary history of the Grail is intimately

connected with the life of the earliest Christian community, its appeal is not limited to believing Christians. The Grail Mysteries have always been, and will always remain, for all of mankind and for all ages in time, for they deal with spiritual realities basic to the human spirit which are everywhere intuitively comprehended and spontaneously loved.

The Holy Grail, according to the legend, was the Cup from which the Lord Christ and His disciples drank at the Last Supper, that holy night in which He gave to them the last and highest teaching of His earthly ministry. One of the sources of this legend is a charming account in verse known as *The Sweet Old Poem of Joseph of Arimathea.*

The legend has it that Joseph of Arimathea was present when Christ Jesus sat for that last hour with His disciples and gave them His farewell blessing. As his memory lingered over the wise words of the Master, Joseph felt that he must have a memorial of that hour so rich in meaning to the world, so he returned to the holy Upper Chamber, there to find the table still standing with the remains of the feast upon it. He joyfully took the Cup from which all had drunk and hid it in the folds of his mantle.

As he stood later in the darkness of Calvary, Joseph still held the Cup in his arms; and when the Roman soldier pierced the Master's side with his lance, Joseph lifted the Cup and caught in it the sacred blood which flowed from the wound. After the Cup had served so holy a purpose it could never fall to any ordinary use. Joseph preserved the Cup with its sacred contents, and it became his guardian and comforter, the Holy Grail.

Joseph later lost his possessions and was thrown into prison where he was left to starve in a high tower, but the Cup was with him, which saved him from all harm. For something like forty years he lingered behind stone walls, but declared afterward that it had seemed to him three days and three nights because the Grail was with him.

He had been condemned to starvation, but the angels spread for him the table of the Grail, and he was fed daily with what he liked best to eat and to drink. His confinement was to be solitary, but glorious winged visitors floated through the stone walls of his prison, bringing him words of heavenly consolation; and the Master whom he had seen hanging upon the cross sat with him for long hours and taught him wisdom he could have learned from no other source. What wonder that the forty years seemed but as three days and three nights!

When the glad hour of freedom came, the Master said: "Son, go thou forth and carry My message to many lands." Then Joseph was sorrowful and replied, "Master, I have always been slow of speech, and I cannot preach," "Son," said the Shining One, with gentle encouragement, "trouble not as to thy words, but open thy lips and speech shall be given thee."

So Joseph left his prison walls and went to the shore of the sea where a white boat carried him to Britain. Then joy came to that land. The great Abbey of Glastonbury was built to hold the Grail. The hawthorn bloomed at Christmas time because the Grail had come, and the nightingale sang in its branches.

To the discerning mind the foregoing incidents are subtle references to certain initiatory experiences that came to St. Joseph of Arimathea. The nature of these experiences will be shown in the following pages.

The legends state that when Joseph left the Holy Land carrying the Grail he also took with him several other sacred objects: the Crown of Thorns, the Spear which pierced the Savior's side, the four Nails, the Dish on which the holy food was served. There were five "hallows" in all, and we shall discover in the *High History of the Holy Grail* that the sacred Cup was known to King Arthur in five different forms, the last of which was the Chalice.

The Holy Grail and the Red Cross

Joseph travelled with an entourage consisting, among others, of Mary Magdalene, Lazarus, Longinus (or Longius, the soldier who thrust the spear into Christ's side), Mary and Martha, and a certain King Evelake whom he converted to Christ in the land of Sarras, "the East." This King Evelake prayed to be allowed to live until one of his lineage might come to serve the Holy Grail; and so in the Grail cycle we find that he still lives three hundred years later, and in the Parsifal cycle of Wagner we know him under the name of Titurel. Upon his white shield the figure of the Crucified had been drawn, but this disappeared and the shield remained blank until the death of the son of Joseph of Arimathea, who, dying, wrote upon it with his blood the sign of a red cross. This shield also was stored away in the "White Abbey" until that one should come who was destined to redeem it. The knight to whom it descended was Galahad, a name meaning "Gilead," as shown in certain Vatican texts where the name Gilead is in fact translated as Galahad.

Thus we may assume from Grail legends that the cross was already known in Britain at the time Constantine saw his vision, became Emperor of Rome and founded his Order of Red Cross Knights. From an early time the red cross was the sign of the martyr and during the Crusades became especially associated with the Order of Templars - and after the destruction of the Order of Templars, with the Order of the Garter and with St. George, the great martyr soldier.

Farther back still we may trace the ancient emblem of the red cross in Masonic legend, where it is shown as under a veil, in fashion of a pantomime, how the staggering steps of the dying Master, Hiram Abiff, describe in blood a cross.* According to Christian esotericists this Master Workman was reborn as Lazarus and raised from the tomb by "the strong grip of the paw of the Lion of Judah."

The archetypal emblem, without embellishments, is the simple equal-armed cross inscribed within a circle, signifying the four quarters of the earth, which the Templars hoped to rule from a central throne at Jerusalem. And throughout Europe, so long as the Kingdom of Jerusalem stood and the Knights Templar were its protectors, so long the belief persisted that these Knights were veritably the Knights of the Holy Grail. After the Kingdom of Jerusalem fell to the Moselms and the Order of the Temple was suppressed (1312), the red cross was taken over by Edward III of England in connection with the Order of the Garter (1344) under

---

*Who Was Hiram Abiff? J.S.M. Ward, M.A., Baskerville Press, London, 1925.

the aegis of St. George, together with the insignia of the red rose. It is of the utmost significance that these "garters" were in fact an ornamental device consisting of a wreath of seven roses on a blue ribbon from which depended an image of St. George.

Another stream of development emerged in Germany, where in 1313, in the year following the downfall of the Templars, the Order of the Rose Cross was founded by Christian Rosenkreuz; the black cross of the Germanic Order of Templars, the Teutonic Knights, entwined by a living rose plant becoming his personal emblem.*

It is said that Joseph's little company did not proceed at once and directly to Britain, however, but stopped first at Marseille, where Joseph was again instructed in a vision to journey still farther west, to Britain. And so it was that he and his company arrived at Glastonbury, where his first act was to build a "little church," in later times known as the Chapel of St. Joseph; and this church was a shrine for the holy Cup, where it was always surrounded and safe-guarded by these holy ones.

> From our old books I know
> That Joseph came of old to Glastonbury
> And there the heathen Prince, Arviragus,
> Gave him an isle of marsh whereon to build;
> And there he built with wattles from the marsh
> A little lonely church in days of yore.
> —Tennyson

Let no one be misled by the words "little church." This "little church" was to house the Christ Mysteries in the Western world, and it endured to challenge the authority of Rome in later centuries despite bitter and cruel persecutions which drove its faithful servants into hiding; and it continually knew and called to itself its own in every century.

This early Greek-speaking British Christianity was on the friendliest footing with the native Druidism, through the mediation of the free Greek spirit which had already found haven in what was the "far west" of that day. It has been said that the

---

*The Rosicrucian Cosmo-Conception, Max Heindel, Oceanside, Calif.

Druids, lacking a written language, first began to write down their doctrines in the Greek characters; and it is understandable that the Druids should have taken up the Greek language which was then the universal mode of communication. There were Greek universities in Gaul, and Marseille itself was a university town, strongly pervaded by the Greek spirit; and the legend is well known that a Pythagorean teacher once taught Orphism to the Druids.

After Joseph of Arimathea had carried the Sacred Cup of the Last Supper, the Sacred Spear and other "hallows" to Britain, his descendants from generation to generation constituted themselves the devoted guardians of the sacred relics, under a vow of harmlessness and absolute purity of thought, word, emotion and deed. For many years the Holy Grail remained in full view of the pilgrims who came to the shrine, and its presence conferred blessings upon the land whose king had given it sanctuary. But at length one of the holy men to whom its guardianship had descended so far forgot the obligation of his sacred office as to look with unhallowed eyes upon a young female pilgrim as she knelt before him. The sacred lance instantly punished his frailty, as it suddenly fell upon him, inflicting a deep wound. This extraordinary wound could by no means be healed, and the guardian of the Holy Grail was ever afterward called "Le Roi Pescheur"—the Sinner King. The Holy Grail withdrew its visible presence from the crowds who came to worship, and an iron age succeeded to the happiness which its presence had diffused among the tribes of Britain.

The ancient home of the Grail was called Avalon, or the Isle of Avalon, because in the early centuries of the Christian era this land was marshy and held a lake. In later times the lake disappeared, and the "Isle of Marsh" became a valley, the Vale of Avalon. Here Joseph and his followers built their "little church," and around it they built twelve small huts in which they lived, praying and meditating, and doing good works for all who came their way.

Joseph of Arimathea, the legends say, left this earth life about the year 85 A.D.

It is from these early times that the White Swan became the

symbol of the Grail Knight, initiated in the Mysteries of the Christ. The Swan, and another aquatic bird, the Pelican, were the emblems of the Christ Truth. The Swan in particular has been from remotest times in the Orient a symbol of Deity and of the Initiate, devotee or yoga, who has achieved liberation in God. In Wagner's music-dramas the Swan motif always announces the coming of a Knight of the Grail. Again we note that the constellation Cygnus, the Swan, is called the Northern Cross and stands upright on the western horizon in the likeness of a Latin cross at its setting.

Whether the Antioch Cup or the Toledo Cup is in fact the cup which garnered the blood of Christ on Golgotha, the esoterics of the history remain unchanged. A Mystery School was founded in Britain by one who is thought to have been Joseph of Arimathea, and this School (or Church) owed no allegiance to Rome.

The weaving of the Arthurian tales into the Grail cycle in the Middle Ages under the patronage of Henry II (father of Richard the Lion-hearted and husband of Eleanor of Aquitaine whose emblem was the Golden Rose) was in truth a return of the English spirit to its spiritual roots in the Christianity of Joseph of Arimathea and the "little church" of Glastonbury. When Henry VII tried to show that his son Arthur was King Arthur returned, he prepared the way for Henry VIII and the English Reformation. English kings under the domination of Rome had tried, and would try again, to stamp out this British Christianity, but repeatedly it arose from the dust into which it was trampled, for its seed was imperishable.

When at last Henry VIII freed the British nation from the dominion of the Bishop of Rome, the enemies of esoteric Christianity imputed shame to a church founded, as they declared, by a king whose only motive was to rid himself of one wife and to take another. What, they demanded, can be expected of a church whose foundations are laid in adultery and murder?—a slander oft repeated in our own day. But the historian of esoteric Christianity reveals the truth: that the foundation of the true and original Church of England was laid by Joseph of Arimathea, who, even as Peter, was instructed by the Christ both before and after His

Crucifixion, and that the authority of Joseph is not to be set aside
by Peter. Nor was it set aside by Peter when Peter himself sat in
the Bishop's Chair at Rome.

Whatever may be the facts about Henry VIII as a human being
and as a king, he acted in this instance as the representative of the
great suppressed Church of his people, and it was by their will, not
his own, that the separation from Rome came about.

Great confusion has arisen from the suppression of the history
of Greek and Druidic Christianity in Britain and Gaul, as well as
the Christianity implanted among the Germanic peoples by
Christian missionaries who were not under allegiance to Rome;
and it is only as we unravel the intricate symbolism of the Grail
legends that something of the truth is once more brought to light,
in these last centuries of the Piscean Age in which "all that is
hidden shall be revealed," when "Elias" comes to restore all
things.

Whether Peter or Joseph was the earlier in Europe the scriptural
and apocryphal documents do not clearly show. The Grail legends,
as we have seen, try to reconcile two differing accounts of
Joseph's arrival in Britain; the one, that he was in prison for three
days and nights, the other that he was in prison for forty years. In
the latter case, if he was imprisoned immediately after the
Crucifixion of the Christ, his release would have come at about the
time when Jerusalem fell to the Romans. We note also that when
it is said that Joseph lost his possessions this would pertain to his
possessions in Judea. But Joseph was a wealthy merchant whose
fleet of ships sailed to the far off places of the world, Britain
among them. There both means and land awaited him and his
companions; or at least as much as was needed for the day and the
way.

The Castle Carbonek

Grail scholars are not in agreement as to the nature and location
of Carbonek, the Castle of the Grail, "the Castle Foursquare." The
stronghold of the Grail and the identity of its kings was as
profound a mystery to the Middle Ages as to the modern. The
Grail, and other hallows, was brought from Jerusalem to Britain,
and the Castle built for their protection. It cannot be proved,

however, that the Castle of the Grail Kings was located at Glastonbury. One tradition has it in the mountains dividing Spain and France and in the care of a "pagan" king who was converted to Christianity. The kings and princes of this dynasty bear fantastic names Arabian in sound. The story is that Sennabor, Prince of Cappadocia, and his three sons, Parille, Azubar and Sabbilar, were with the Emperor Vespasian at the time of the seige of Jerusalem by the Roman legions. Parille married the daughter of Vespasian—Argusilla or Orgusille—at Rome and received lands in France, while to Azubar and Sabbilar went Anjou and Cornwall. The son of Parille and Argusilla was named Titurisone, "the stem of the Grail-race," who became king after the death of his father (who was poisoned) and married Elizabeth of Arragonia (Aragon). Titurisone's son was Titurel, the first of the Grail dynasty proper. Titurel ruled over precisely those areas which later were important in the stories of the Swan Knights: Provence, Arles, Lotharingia, Auvergne and Navarre.

The site on which to build the Castle of the Holy Grail was revealed to Titurel by an angel, a remote spot high in the Pyrenees, safe from intrusion, guarded on every side by natural barriers of mountain and stream. Men labored on the sacred structure during the day; angels carried the labor forward in the hours of the night; and so the holy house was built. The castle was three or four hundred years in building and Titurel still lived; he founded a dynasty, marrying Richonde, a holy maiden who was the daughter of a Spanish king. The elder of their two sons, Frimutel by name, succeeded his father Titurel, and the eldest of Frimutel's five children was Amfortas. Among the daughters of the Grail dynasty was Herzeliede who became the mother of Parsifal, and Urepanse, the mother of Prester John.

After Parsifal became king, Titurel retired to India (a term anciently meaning the Far East generally and including Persia), where he died. Parsifal ruled for ten (or twelve) years, and after the murder of his son Lohengrin he too returned to Asia. Titurel seems to be the King Evelake of the English narratives.

The fact that this account ascribes the earliest origins of the Grail dynasty to Cappadocia, the home of St. George, explains the insistent inclusion of St. George in the Grail histories.

Yet the relationship of the Grail Castle and its dynasty to Glastonbury remains obscure. The dynasty appears to be closely associated with Glastonbury Abbey, which is almost certainly the White Abbey mentioned in the Grail cycles. It was at the "White Abbey" that Galahad's white shield hung, bearing the red cross inscribed upon it in blood by Joseph.

Joseph's little church and community were on a marshland; Carbonek is far otherwise. In Tennyson's *Idylls of the King* it is Lancelot who gives us the description:

> *Behold the enchanted towers of Carbonek*
> *A castle like a rock upon a rock*
> *With chasm-like portals open to the sea,*
> *And steps that met the breaker! There was none*
> *Stood near it but a lion on each side*
> *That kept the entry.*

In this passage Tennyson describes only the lions which guard the Grail, symbolic of the Lion of the tribe of Judah, but we find elsewhere that the peacock is frequently shown, together with the lion, as, for example, in the Abbey paintings in the Boston Public Library. In primitive Christianity the peacock was emblematic of the glorified human soul, but in pagan antiquity it was a symbol of royalty. In some sects the peacock is the symbol of Lucifer, who should be redeemed and restored to his throne by the Messiah, according to kabbalistic lore.

Lancelot describes the Castle of Carbonek most vividly, together with the Grail sanctuary which occupies its tallest eastern tower:

> *. . .nothing in the sounding hall I saw*
> *No bench nor table, painting on the wall*
> *Or shield of knight, only the rounded moon*
> *Thro' the tall oriel on the rolling sea.*
> *But always in the quiet house I heard,*
> *Clear as a lark, high o'er me as a lark,*
> *A sweet voice singing in the topmost tower*
> *To the eastward. Up I climbed a thousand steps*
> *With pain; as in a dream I seemed to climb*
> *Forever; at the last I reached the door. . .*

In the Abbey pictures one observes that the artist shows the architectural style of the early Christian type Romanesque, not Gothic. But the Grail epics surviving today come from the medieval period when the great Gothic cathedrals were being built throughout Europe and the Isles. We therefore find, for instance, in some Grail legends, that the Grail Castle is a typical Gothic structure, with pinnacles and spires, and that upon the spire which rises above the towered sanctuary there is a ruby surmounted by a crystal cross. This calls to mind that Paracelsus said that the element Azoth was a "stone or crystal" which possessed magnetic properties and which had the power to cure diseases.

There has been much speculation as to the actual location of the Grail Castle, especially in the Middle Ages. The hill called Glastonbury Tor is said to be one of the "hollow mountains" often mentioned in fairy tales, with channels leading to the center of the earth; and it is possible that this may be the original site of the Grail Castle, although Chalice Hill, from its name, would seem to have distinct associations in this direction as well. Or perhaps, like the city of Lyonesse which is prominent in the story of Sir Tristram (it was there he met his death), Carbonek now lies sunken under the waters of the Atlantic Ocean. Or. contrariwise, the rocky site which once "chasm-like met the sea" may as suggested be the present Glastonbury with its two sacred hills, now remote from the waters. As one part of the land sinks, another part rises in the great geological epochs of our planet. The whereabouts of the Castle Carbonek, Grail stronghold and Castle of its kings remains to be discovered.

The Legend of Lucifer and the Emerald Grail

One of the earliest accounts of the origin of the Emerald Grail to be found in the English language describes a war in heaven in which Lucifer fought with the Archangel Michael, and we are told that as Lucifer was cast headlong from heaven the glorious emerald of his crown fell into the abyss. It was rescued by angels and from it was formed the Cup of the Last Supper in which the Savior pledged His blood to His disciples and in which it was caught by Joseph of Arimathea on Golgotha.

Perhaps reminiscent of this legend is the hexagonal green dish preserved for centuries in the Church of St. Laurence at Genoa. This large dish is shaped roughly like the calyx of a flower, and was thought to be the dish on which the pasqual lamb was served at the Last Supper. Supposedly carved from a single huge emerald it was proved to be simple green glass when it was accidentally broken in the time of Napoleon I. It was taken by the Crusaders at the seige of Caesarea, in 1101, and came originally from a mosque at Antioch.

Green is in the East the color of wisdom, but Lucifer's crown held other jewels besides this great emerald. The crown jewel in Lucifer's crown was called Morning Star. By the multitude this was taken to mean Venus. By the initiated it was understood to signify Mercury, which is also a Morning Star, but one which is almost invisible to the naked eye and must be sought for diligently in its bright place close to the sun.

When Lucifer and his angels, says an ancient kabbalistic text, were expelled from heaven the seats left vacant were reserved for human souls. It is also said that the great work of the Messiah is to restore Lucifer to his throne in all the glory which he had in the beginning, and that when this is done, all the sins of mankind will be blotted out as if they had never been. It was to accomplish the redemption of Lucifer and Satan (Death and Hades) that Christ spent three days in the tomb. From which it would seem that the Hebrew and early Christian occultists saw a very close connection between the fallen angels and mankind, in which both were to be saved by the Messiah.

The peacock and lion shown in the Abbey paintings in the Boston Public Library may also refer to the redemption of Lucifer, in the light of this very ancient tradition.

Addison writes in *The Spectator* (1714): "I was once engaged in discourse with a Rosicrucian about the Great Secret. He talked of the secret as of a spirit which lived within an emerald, and converted everything that was near it to the highest perfection that it was capable of. 'It gives a lustre,' says he, 'to the sun and water to the diamond. It irradiates every metal and enriches lead pain and care and melancholy from the person on whom it falls. In short, its presence naturally changes every place into a kind of heaven.' After he had gone on for some time in this unintelligible cant, I found that he jumbled natural and moral ideas together into the same discourse, and that his great secret was nothing else than content."

Contentment, or tranquillity of mind, may well be a fruitage of the true spiritual alchemy, but it would be a mistake to think that this is all that is intended. The reference is to the solving of the problem ("great secret") of good and evil, which resides in the mind, and is the secret of the mind, or the "maya" of the orientalist. Goethe's "Emerald Serpent" and the "Emerald Rainbow" about the throne of God in Revelation have a similar connotation.

The star Venus was anciently associated with Adonis, the Morning Star rising in a wine-red sea of light. Every Mystery School has a legend of the cleansing blood of a dying Savior who is usually a god or demi-god. The blood of the dying Adonis produced the scarlet anemone of Lebanon. The blood of Attis shone through the blue of the violet. The blood of John the Baptist dyed red the pale petals of the wild rose. The blood of Dionysus flowed in the purple-red juice of the grape. Among gems the ruby symbolizes the saving blood and is therefore called the Stone of Christianity. It symbolizes the concept of the Savior (Pharaoh) of whom it is said in the Pyramid Texts: "Thou didst not depart dead, but thou didst depart living."

With red as the color of life, green is the color of life in the earth, the calyx in which the blossom is inclosed and which becomes the vessel bearing the seeds of future embodiments. In Greece, long before Christ, the death and resurrection of nature was symbolized in the Eleusinian Mysteries, where the "ear of corn" (sheath of wheat) of the goddess Demeter was reverenced; and in Egypt an image of Osiris was shown from which green leaves sprouted. According to Egyptian myth also "the goddess of heaven, striding across the sky, strews far and wide the green, luminous pebbles of emerald, malachite and turquoise which becomes stars and planets." (Pyramid Text Commentary).

The Egyptians also believed that when the sun travelled through the underworld during the night hours it was green. Hence the green sun would symbolize the midnight sun of Egypt, and show at the same time that as the sun always arises in the morning so the spirit always rises from the death of the body and is reborn.

The Emerald Grail has enjoyed continuing popularity in modern esotericism, yet the Grail of the Parsifal of Wolfram von Eschenbach is a Stone, in color garnet and hyacinth (red-purple), and Wagner describes his Grail as a chalice of crimson and purple hue. So also Tennyson in his "Idylls" says, 'the Holy Grail, rose-red with beatings in it as if alive."

Wolfram wrote that the Stone was left behind upon the earth by angels (not necessarily "fallen") when they returned to paradise. Enoch says that certain angels "fell" because they overstayed their time on earth and were not able to rejoin their celestial comrades.

Again we read in the Zohar that the four primary colors are red, green, white (in which yellow is hidden) and sapphire. Red, green and white are everywhere associated together in the Grail talismans, as also in alchemy.

A discovery of recent years throws added light on these symbolisms. In 1955 the caretaker of the Garden of the Tomb at Jerusalem, the supposed Tomb of Joseph of Arimathea in which Christ was buried, was tidying up loose rubble piled against the foot of the cliff on the left side of the Tomb, when he found a metal box in which was a richly jewelled ornament. This was a cross set with twelve rubies against a background of sun with golden rays, with a crown above it holding five green stones, and with a white bird below it brooding over seven little birds as in a nest, and with a semi-circle of eleven white stones at the base. Two pieces of metal, like the legs of a compass, appear to meet somewhere behind the central ornament of cross and sunburst. The crown with green stones may quite possibly suggest Lucifer's crown.

Many persons supposed that because this artifact was found outside Joseph's tomb it must go back to the early Christian era; but the Tomb and Garden show evidence of having been entered at many different times, and some scientists date the ornament no more than one hundred fifty to two hundred years ago. However, the scientists are not in complete agreement, and the jewel may be much older. If it is no more than two hundred years old, it dates from the renaissance of Rosicrucianism and Masonry in the eighteenth century.

We have said that as the color of blood is associated with the Grail, the red cross also occurs repeatedly throughout Christian history. When the Garden Tomb was unearthed, two Byzantine crosses were found inscribed in red on the east wall. These have faded away on exposure to light and air, but copies of them were made and are reproduced in the various brochures dealing with this discovery.

THE HOLY GRAIL

The Mystery of the Holy Grail
Doth to the seeking soul avail
To give a knowledge of the Plan,
The Mystery of the Christ and Man.

An occult legend says the Cup
From out of which our Lord did sup
Was fashioned from a precious stone
Which fell upon the earth, alone,
Out of the crown of Lucifer
When He to Heaven would not defer.
And this same Cup the blood received
When on the Cross the Christ did bleed,
Then to the western world 'twas brought
By Angels who God's will have wrought.

The intellect doth represent
What Lucifer did man present,
The mind developed in the West
To know the outer world the best.
Yet doth it not suffice, this gift
Alone, unless the man doth lift
His gaze up to the Cross of Christ
Whose blood for man was sacrificed.
Thus is the Grail no empty thing
But bearer for what Christ did bring,
Eternal LIFE, defeating Death,
Made Living by the Spirit's breath.
The Spirit is the Source of Life,
The boundless Light, the Cosmic Life;
When this the intellect receives
New Cosmic Truth it then conceives.
Then doth the mind, the Grail, become
A HOLY Vessel for the SUN (SON).

Behind the Grail is seen the Cross,
It tells us not to count as loss
A seeming failure which in time
Doth prove a Deed the most sublime.
                              —Beredene Jocelyn

Chapter II

AN HISTORICAL ACCOUNT

OF THE ARTHURIAN LEGENDS

The story of the historical King Arthur began approximately fourteen centuries ago. He is said to have lived 500 A.D., or a little earlier, and is thought to have been a leader of the Britons in their battles against the invading Anglo-Saxons. He was evidently so wise a leader and performed so many deeds of valor that he became a hero to his countrymen for all time. Many wonderful legends have grown up to add to the luster of his memory, and he has been credited with possessing all manner of supernatural powers. A chronicler describes him as "one of Love's lovers," and says that "his famous deeds are right fit to be kept in remembrance."

During the eleventh, twelfth, thirteenth and fourteenth centuries the Arthurian legends attained the height of their popularity. Minstrels and troubadours carried the fame of Arthur over all of Europe, celebrating his glorious deeds in song. Historians told of them in prose and poets in verse, while artists adorned the halls, tapestries and stained glass windows of many castles with scenes depicting the marvelous exploits of King Arthur and his knights. There were many who believed that Arthur had never died but had become a sort of guardian angel for his people, watching over them from his home in the fairy Isle of Avalon, and that in times of acute crisis he would return to lead England to victory.

It was about 1136 that the Arthurian legends began to assume tangible literary form. At this time Geoffrey of Monmouth wrote his *History of the Kings of Britain,* in which some of Arthur's heroic deeds are described.

In the interim 1175 to 1205, Layamon, a priest of Worcestershire, gave the first presentation in the English language of the Arthurian story. This was written in verse, wherein Arthur says: "I will fare to Avalon, to the fairest of all maidens, to Argante the Queen, an elf most fair, and she shall make my wounds all sound—make me all whole with healing draughts. And afterwards I will come again to my kingdom and dwell with the Britons with mickle joy."

Perhaps the supreme masterpiece dealing with the legends of Arthur is that which was written by Sir Thomas Malory in his famous *Morte d' Arthur.* Here we find chivalry and romance portrayed at its highest and best, with background of feudal grandeur.

Malory wrote his great work while he was in prison during the War of the Roses (1455-1486). It achieved an enormous popularity and revived throughout the English-speaking world a vivid interest in the life of Arthur, his kingly deeds and the deeds of his noble knights.

In the year that Malory's book was published, added interest was imparted to the subject by reason of the announcement of England's new king, Henry VII of the house of Tudor, that he himself had descended from King Arthur, and that in his son, whom he named Arthur, Merlin's prophecy had come true—Arthur had returned.

The Round Table, which at present adorns the wall in Winchester Castle, was decorated as we see it today on the occasion of the birth of Prince Arthur, and in his honor. However, the origins and first usage of the Round Table lie far in the historic past, when "Round Tables" and court circles of thirteen were numerous and represented the established traditions, both religious and civil, of the country before the days of Christianity and before there were any Christian kings.

In the sixteenth century, during the reign of Elizabeth I, Arthurian pageantry was one of the most popular forms of entertainment at Court. Many of the famous writers of the time introduced characters from the *Arthurian Fantasies* into their works, as, for example, Edmund Spencer in his *Faerie Queen.* The first Arthurian play in English, Thomas Hughes' *Misfortunes of Arthur,* was presented before the Queen in 1588.

By this time, however, a heavy pall of materialism was descending upon the world—a materialism that endeavored to substitute "reason and common sense" for the chivalry and romance of King Arthur's Court. These beautiful legends were gradually cast aside by the mass mind. Their supernatural aspects were relegated to the category of "old wives' tales." Only in the minds and hearts of mystic poets and artists they lingered on like some half-forgotten dream.

It was due largely to Lord Tennyson, England's poet laureate under Queen Victoria, that the nineteenth century saw a renaissance of the Arthurian tales. Tennyson was deeply inspired by Malory's *Morte d' Arthur, and upon its themes he based his great mystical and philosophical epic, Idylls of the King.* This work was published in 1842 and was unprecedentedly popular in all English-speaking countries, as exemplified especially in the United States where by 1890 these poems were taught in all public schools, and where also the aristocratic ruling families of the South actually endeavored to make chivalry a way of life. Sir Walter Scott's novels of medieval chivalry furnished the prose accompaniment to the poetic passion of idealism which swept England and America with Tennyson's poetic epic; while on the continent Richard Wagner brought forth his astonishing and revolutionary music-dramas based on similar medieval themes.

In the twentieth century the Arthurian and Grail poems have again suffered a relapse from popularity, except, as before, among dedicated mystics for whom their charm has been perennial. We have not seen the end of the Holy Grail, nor of its avowed servitors. Although these stories and poems are couched in the words and customs of the West, a whole new audience awaits them in the Orient. Indian scholars and mythographers say that the story of the Last Supper and the search for the Grail has many parallels in Indian legend, most of which arose from historic episodes or from the religious beliefs and rites of the people; but which also include a distinct branch of literature arising from Western sources by way of Christians who fled from persecution in the west and found sanctuary in India. The "Thomas Christians" of the Malabar coast are among these.

Indian scholars point out that the general framework of the Holy Grail legend always postulates the existence of a magic cup or other talisman and a land which is suffering famine and dearth by reason of the sin or weakness of the king, who is in reality the embodiment of a nature god. When the nature god was sick, nature was sick also, the crops suffered, famine struck the land, the people sickened and died. Then a folk hero seeks for the magic talisman to restore the king's health and with it the prosperity of land and people. One usually finds that there is a magic drink of some kind, because water is necessary to restore a parched land, and it is not unusual to find that it is a heroine rather than a hero who is called to the Quest.

The omnipresence of the Grail motif in all civilizations, and as far back as there is any record, attests to its universal significance and promises the world-wide restoration of the Grail Mystery, probably in some not far-distant day.

It is to be understood that in one sense the true Grail is the epic or legend itself and that the magic which it holds is the Esoteric Doctrine of the people to whom the legends are conveyed. That some international poet will one day write a story of the Buddha, showing him as setting out in quest of the Grail and attaining it under the Bodhi-tree, as Galahad finds his Tree of Paradise in Sarras, is, indeed, inevitable. There are seven Schools of the Lesser Mysteries, and each of these Schools must of necessity have its own "Cup" (instruction) which confers the magic powers of Illumination and Initiation. Why recast the Esoteric Doctrine into new forms of poetry? Why is not the ancient prose sufficient, one might ask. It must be realized that the most perfect instruction deserves the most perfect art form that can convey or communicate it to others; as the perfect jewel deserves the perfect setting which only a master craftsman is able to create.

The Arthurian legend continued that after the grievous wound which Arthur received at the hands of Modred, the evil and traitorous knight, he was taken to an old church wherein hung a broken cross, and that there he died at midnight and was buried in the little churchyard by his few faithful followers. Another legend relates that he was rescued by the Three Beautiful Queens and carried away to the fairy Isle of Avalon, where he still lives and rules, awaiting the time when he can return to serve again upon the earth. The two legends are complementary: the one relates to the body, the other to the soul of the great King.

The ruined church and broken cross symbolize the fact that the Church has discarded and forgotten the high initiatory teachings which formed the cornerstone of Christianity in the first three hundred years after Christ.

After the building in England of Glastonbury Abbey, some of the priests who ministered there declared that it had been their high privilege to receive the disinterred bodies of both King Arthur and his beautiful Queen Guinevere, and that these had been buried under the High Altar in the church. The Queen, however, was not laid at the side of the King as his equal. She had been placed at the feet of the King, for she had wounded him sorely in life.

Tradition preserved the memory of the place of Arthur's interment within the Abbey, as we are told by Giraldus Cambrensis, who was present when the grave was opened by command of Henry II about the year 1150, and saw the bones and sword of the monarch, and a leaden cross set into his tombstone upon which was the inscription in rude Roman letters: "Here lies buried the famous King Arthur, in the island Avalonis."

Chapter III

THE COMING OF ARTHUR

Each earth life is a day in God's great school. As it requires many days to complete a college course and reach the glad day of graduation, so it requires many earth lives in which to learn all the lessons this planet has to teach the evolving ego. It is only when all earth lessons have been learned that the ego, or human spirit, attains liberation from the wheel of birth and death.

There are, however, some few advanced souls who have forged ahead far beyond their fellow-men and, having attained liberation from this earth sphere, they return as great Master Teachers when mankind, by reason of the blindness of ignorance, creates some great crisis requiring special assistance. These advanced beings are known as the Compassionate Ones, and it is of these that King Arthur is the perfect type-pattern.

Such high souls have always responded to humanity's urgent plea for help since the earliest dawn of civilization. When their mission is ended their departure has always been characterized by the promise with which King Arthur concluded his life work: "I go, but I will come again." This promise has been given to mankind by all World Teachers, even including the most sublime of Masters when, as the disciples stood looking up into heaven after the Ascension, the angels said: "As ye have seen Him go, so He shall return."

The esotericist knows that history cannot be truly written without an understanding of the Intelligences working behind the scenes of human evolution, who see many centuries in advance when a crisis in the life of the human race approaches, and long before the hour strikes, the mighty forces of spiritual hosts are drawn up to do battle with evil, and powerful, spiritually-minded Leaders are awaiting their call to rebirth. The paths of history are touched to gold where these Great Ones have passed, and when in later times their deeds are reduced to writing, something of magic still lingers, even upon the dullest of pages. But mystics and poets are not deceived by the uninspired phrases of materialistic historians, and in legend and art the spiritual truth sings again.

Initiated troubadours have told the poetic truth about Arthur and his Table Round. They say that Arthur came from the fairy island of Avalon, the land of the "Little People." This is a reference to the inner or etheric realm, for it is here that the nature spirits—the "little gods"—make their home. Arthur was brought to the earth plane by "Three Beautiful Queens" who bore the names of Faith, Hope and Love. These are the qualities which always mark the life of a World Teacher when he comes to earth on a mission of mercy.

The poet tells us that one night there appeared before Merlin, the wise, in the midst of a great storm at sea, "a ship, the shape thereof a dragon winged, and all from stem to stern bright with shining people on the decks, gone as soon as seen. Then mighty waves came in, each mightier than the last—a ninth one, gathering half the deep, and full of voices, slowly rose, plunged roaring in, with all the wave aflame. And down the wave and in the flame was borne a naked babe that rode to Merlin's feet. He stopped and caught the babe and cried, 'The King!' Then round him rose the sea so that he and the child were clothed in fire."

On every holy night thereafter, in a strange heavenly light, there appeared a wonderful ship, shaped like a dragon, filled with a celestial people.

A more vivid, poetic account of the birth of a hold child would be difficult to find in the whole range of literature. The wise physician in attendance upon the holy mother, the three wise women bearing the symbolic titles of fundamental virtue, the ship, or brightly gleaming aureole in which the spirit of the babe rode slowly into its earthly incarnation, the glad cry of recognition when the infant is safely delivered—all this the poet conveys in the most exquisite of spiritual symbolism, touched with the fire of the divinely illumined imagination.

In the glory which surrounded the babe the wondrous story of the master-life shone revealed to the vision of Merlin; he knew this babe from lives lived on earth before when, as now, they labored together in the Cause of Light. Nine waves brought the babe to the earth; nine Initiations through which that ego had passed in former times, and which now he came to reestablish in this new outpost of advancing life.

So also we read that Merlin on a certain occasion went out to sea *in a ship of glass* with *nine Lords.*

The Church Fathers who wrote and taught during the first three centuries after Christ referred frequently to the work of the Mysteries and the important part which they occupied in the teachings of the early Christian community.

The work of the Essenes was also centered in these Mysteries. The Essenes were a holy sect whose work in Palestine was an endeavor to prepare mankind for the First Coming of the greatest of all World Teachers. The work of the modern "Grail Knight" is again centered in the Mysteries, as his most important task is to assist in preparing humanity for the Second Coming of the Supreme World Master.

When Arthur reached young manhood he possessed a rare beauty of countenance and supernatural spiritual powers unequalled in his time. One night, in a dream-vision, he was taken into the holy Chapel of St. Joseph of Arimathea, at Carbonek. There he saw the Grail ever guarded by a circle of virgins. There he took part in the Midnight Holy Communion and saw the wondrous spiritual powers of the holy vessel, and there received into his life-long keeping a pure white crystal cross, while a Voice said: "Under this sign will you serve and by this sign you will conquer." Thus he came forth with life pledged to the service of the Grail.

In medieval accounts of the Castle of the Holy Grail we read that it was a Gothic structure topped by a spire, and that on the spire was a great ruby, and upon the ruby a crystal cross such as we first meet here in the story of Arthur.

No doubt historians would say that the story of Arthur's vision of the cross is a retroversion by medieval writers to the story of Constantine's vision; but there can be no proof either way. Both are legends. It is possible that Constantine's vision was suggested by an earlier tradition from Glastonbury, as we have said in another place.

Another famous incident in the Arthurian cycle is that in which Arthur proves his right to the throne. He was shown a great white stone in the center of which a sword had been thrust up to its hilt, and he heard the words spoken: "Only he is worthy to be king who can draw this sword from this stone." He saw many knights attempt the feat—but always the sword remained immovable. At last Arthur laid his hand upon it, and it came forth readily. Even so do spiritual powers remain embedded in "Stone" until the time is ripe for their use, when they come forth easily, as the sword came to the hand of Arthur.

There is a very beautiful symbolism in this incident of the sword, and it is found many times throughout the various medieval legends, always holding the same mystery. We shall meet with it again in the Idyll of Sir Galahad, who draws his sword from a *red* stone floating in a river. There is a suggestion here that Galahad is in fact the one destined to succeed Arthur, supplanting Modred, the failed Prince who, through Arthur's son, was not in line to inherit.

Esoterically the stone typified that which is crystallized and unchangeable. In other words, it typifies the Old Order of the Ages. The sword is the Spirit of Truth which the worthy pioneer must always be able to extricate from the Old and to use in cutting his way through the obstacles that would hinder his progress as he passes into the New.

Chapter IV

THE ROUND TABLE: TRAINING FOR KNIGHTHOOD

It has often been said that the origins of the Round Table are lost amid the shadows of antiquity. It is well known that the earliest tournaments of medieval times were sometimes referred to as "round tables."

A late representation of Arthur's Round Table consists of twenty-four alternating white and green bands, in the center of which is emblazoned a large red rose in whose heart appears a half-opened rose of pearly white. Historians assure us that this particular table—which hangs in Winchester Castle—originates with the Tudor kings, whose colors were red and white, harmonizing the conflicting loyalties of the formerly warring houses of Lancaster and York. But the esoteric Christian understands that the red and white roses have always borne an important symbolism in the spiritual life of mystic and occultist alike. In the early days of the Christian community, each aspirant was taught that he must come to change the passion-filled blood into the purity and high spiritual attainment, typified by the rose, both red and white; just as we saw that the spire of the Gothic Grail Castle was tipped with a blazing ruby surmounted by a crystal cross.

Arthur's seat was at the head of the Table, and it is said that the King founded the Round Table so "that when his fair fellowship sat to meat, their chairs should be high alike, their services equal, and none before or after his comrade." It is an early legend which says that the Table was made in likeness of the Table used at the Last Supper. The seats which surrounded the Table were thirteen in number, a numerical pattern of significance. Twelve only of these seats could be occupied, and they only by knights of the highest fame; the thirteenth represented the seat of the traitor Judas. It remained always empty. It was called the Perilous Seat, since the time when a rash and haughty Saracen knight had dared to seat himself in it and the earth had opened and swallowed him up.

A magic power wrote upon each seat the name of the knight who was entitled to sit in it. None could succeed to a vacant chair unless he surpassed in valor and glorious deeds the knight who had occupied it before him; lacking this qualification he would be violently repulsed by a hidden force. Thus proof was made of all those who presented themselves to replace the Companions of the Order who had fallen.

Esoterically, this means that every aspirant to spiritual unfoldment is tested and tried before being given the instruction that will unfold his latent, but ripening, powers. Not the Order, or members of the Order, forbid any candidate from assuming a place, but the hidden, titanic forces of his own character forcibly eject him from the midst of spiritual Mysteries for which he is not yet ready or "ripened."

The Seige Perilous, the most dangerous because the focus of the most powerful cosmic forces is for the purest and strongest. It typifies that straight and narrow Path which many search for but few find,—and of those who find, how few follow to its end! The Seige Perilous therefore remains vacant awaiting the coming of the knight who, in the words of St. Paul, has finished the course, has kept faith. This perfect knight is represented in the Arthurian legends by Sir Galahad, who when he first dedicated himself to the Seige Perilous, said: "It is here that I must renounce all things in order that I may gain all." In these words Galahad gave utterance to one of the fundamental maxims of occultism.

When Galahad had triumphed spiritually his name flashed in golden light across the vacant chair, and the angels sang triumphantly above it, joyously proclaiming that Galahad had been found worthy to be numbered among the Companions. The peace, reverence and beauty which permeate the atmosphere of the Mystery School are congenial to the visits of angelic servitors who come and go in the holy environs in the course of their earth ministrations; for in such places there is a vortex of force, with quietness at its center,. which joins heaven and earth, making possible continuous intercommunication between men and angels.

White and green were the heraldic colors of King Arthur. These are the true Life colors, and they are the colors of the exalted Hierarchy of celestial beings who work through the forces of the sign Cancer, the sign of the Celestial Madonna, the Cosmic Mother. Throughout the Mystery literature of antiquity we come upon references to the Sacred Green, which, while notable in Druidic Mysteries, goes back also into the early roots of Esoteric Christianity as it came out of Egypt and the East.

The aspirant in every Mystery School, whether this school be of the Orient or the Occident—there are seven of these Schools in all, each one teaching the Nine Lesser Mysteries—must learn the basic lesson of purity and harmlessness. These are the prerequisites to all true enlightenment. The body must be sustained with pure foods, the mind with pure thoughts, and the life filled with high unselfish deeds. Such were the preparatory steps which led the Grail Knight to King Arthur's Court and to a predestined seat at the Table Round. The vow with which the knight made his allegiance was in substance as follows: "Think pure, speak true, right wrongs, live in fellowship—love only one maiden and cleave to her so long as life shall last."

But the years of preparation leading to this much-sought goal were years of trial, of hardship, of prolonged and dedicated labor of body and mind and soul. While the pattern is that which is usual to the time and the civilization in which the feudal institutions dominated Europe, there is discernible throughout a parallel with the actual occult development of the human being, not only as from childhood to adulthood but also as from spiritual incapacity to spiritual power and understanding. There is evidence here of a profound wisdom which continued to assert its power in the lives of the people, even when it had been driven underground by the aggression of self-seeking States and the Church.

In all Mystery Schools *occult* anatomy has been an important part of Temple teachings, for there the biblical statement, "Ye are the temple of the living God," is taken literally and observed religiously. Every aspirant has been taught to reverence his physical temple and to endeavor to make it a more fitting and responsive instrument for the use of the divine spirit dwelling within it. The life of the body proceeds in seven-year terms, with certain qualities and powers maturing within each period, and with each stage overlapping and complementing and stimulating the growth of the next. The seventh period of growth ends with the forty-ninth year, which concludes the normal course of karmic indebtedness from past incarnations on earth; with the fiftieth year the ego enters upon a period in which, in a special sense, he is instituting new causation, destined to mature in future lives, while extracting the essence of the karma of the life now drawing to a close. This, at least, is true of the spiritually awakened ego; although for the ego which is still in bondage to the flesh, the declining years of an incarnation merely lead to deeper and deeper sleep, which ends in death.

The secret Wisdom which still operated in medieval Europe through initiated singers and teachers led to a plan of life which to a degree paralleled the real, occult growth of the human personality from stage to stage in its septenary cycles.

At the age of seven the sons of nobles who were found to be amenable to knightly training were taken from the homes of their parents and placed in the care of certain Preceptor-Knights. These Preceptor-Knights were noblemen who turned over their great castles and estates to be used as training schools for young knights. Here they underwent strenuous physical training and were taught moral precepts having their foundation in deep spirituality. The first or infant stage was that of Knave, during which the boy was taught to serve in kitchens; the next was Page (seven to fourteen) when he was taught to wait upon the tables and to perform other menial duties which were, however, less menial than those of the Knave.

All this so that they might learn true humility of spirit and the real joy of simplicity in everyday living, as well as to understand how to deal with their own servitors in the years to come.

During their leisure hours the young pages were taught to dance and to play upon the harp, and they learned many other graceful and courtly accomplishments.

It is to be noted that among their more serious studies was an investigation of the mysteries of the forests and streams. The exoteric historian looks upon this as mere excursions in hunting and fishing, and so it was with those who were ready for nothing more. But for the gentle and intelligent lads who showed to the eye of the spiritual Master an aptitude for wisdom, there was something deeper. For in the depths of the dense forests which covered Europe in the Middle Ages there still dwelt certain Masters of the suppressed Wisdom; and to these the superior lads were taken for instruction. These Masters and their Schools were not in all instances "pagans" or "heathens"—but in the eyes of Rome they were assuredly "heretics." How frequently one finds that a Grail hero seeks out, or is sought out, by a "Hermit" dwelling in a wood, who instructs him in heavenly wisdom!

Thus certain favored youths learned to know the various ranks of nature spirits, and the times to invoke the lordly angels, and how the interior eye was to be awakened, what herbs were useful in healing and what was to be learned from their "younger brothers" of sky and forest and stream who "talked" to them and instructed them in the mysteries of divination.

The many "enchanters" who are described in the various knightly legends as possessing superhuman powers which they used for good or ill, as the case might be, represent those persons who by reason of their clairvoyant powers were able to communicate with the nature spirits, the invisible denizens of woodland and field, and thus to direct the course of nature. Both King Arthur and the magician Merlin possessed these powers, which enabled them to live not merely as men among men but as spirits among spiritual beings.

At the age of fourteen the Page became the Esquire. Here his training became strenuous and his duties arduous. He was taught to run foot races, to leap great ditches, scale high walls, to fence, and to vault both on and off a horse while wearing heavy armor; and certain duties were laid upon him to test his integrity and intelligence.

In all of the training castles for the young knights there dwelt many beautiful young maidens under instruction by the Lady of the castle, and each Esquire was encouraged to choose one to be the mistress of his heart, upon whom to bestow all the graceful knightly courtesies which the Lady taught him. For this was the province of the Lady, as the feats of arms and skill in statecraft were the province of the Master-Knight. Hence it was that love, constancy and a high ideal of womanhood were taught as an essential part of the early training in the ways of knighthood.

The young Esquire's proficiency in all manner of graceful horsemanship was continued together with instruction in the social arts of dancing and harp-playing and conversation. He now also learned to sing many of the beautiful ballads which had been composed by the earliest troubadours.

At the age of twenty-one the knightly instruction—physical, moral and mental—was thought to be complete, and the young man was now ready to receive the initiation of knighthood. The preparation for this initiation was solemn and reverent. Many days were spent in fasting and many nights in long vigils of prayer. At length the prospective Knight received the Sacrament, together with the blessing of the priest, at which time also a special blessing and dedication of his sword was made, that it might be used always and only to serve high and noble purposes.

Then the young Knight—or neophyte, in the spiritual sense—was robed in garments of pure white, and brought into the presence of his Preceptor—Knight. This ceremony took place either in a church or in the private chapel of the castle where the training took place. Here, as the young man knelt before the Preceptor-Knight, he was questioned as to his ideals and purposes in assuming knighthood. If the answers proved satisfactory to the presiding Knight, the various articles which constituted the knightly equipment, which were generally in the possession of his chosen maiden, were now presented to him. Among these were the shield, the helmet, the gauntlet and the visor, the spurs and the coat of mail. Last he received his dedicated sword. He then knelt again before the presiding Knight, who gave him the accolade, consisting of three strokes with the flat of a sword — one upon each shoulder and one upon the neck, accompanied by the words: "In the name of God, of St. Michael and St. George, I make thee a knight; be valiant, courteous and loyal!" Then he received his helmet, his shield and spear, and thus the investiture ended.

The years of training for knighthood were complete, and the young knight was now ready to go forth into the world, into adventurous years filled with chivalry, roseate with dreams of romance, yet withal imbued with high spiritual intent and purpose.

PART II

INITIATORY CYCLES

Chapter V

KING ARTHUR'S COURT: A MYSTERY SCHOOL

The Court of King Arthur was, as we have seen, the continuation of an early Christian Mystery School. The Court met annually at Pentecost in one or another of four great Castles: at Camelot, Caerleon, Winchester and Windsor. Camelot was the most celebrated of the four.

The knights who came to the King to dedicate themselves in his service and eventually to the search for the Holy Grail were in truth dedicating themselves to the Christ of the Mysteries. Their aspiration was to achieve spiritual wisdom and to demonstrate anew the far-reaching powers of the Immortal Twelve.

At the inmost heart of chivalry was the Mystery of the Lady, whose image the King bore on his banner, for, contrary to accepted opinion, there is much to show that Lady-worship goes back farther than the Middle Ages, although the Middle Ages gave the cult a new form and a new impetus.

The reverence for the Lady goes back in fact to the cult of the great Mother Goddess, which has always been the basic love-cult of the nations and the ages. Even the patriarchal society of Hebrew Palestine could not wholly expunge it, and in the Kabbala, as well as in the Wisdom literature of the Bible the Divine Feminine peeps as through a veil in the likeness of Isis, Mother of Wisdom, in the mystery of Shekinah, "She who inspires the Prophets." Wherever men meditate on high and holy things, says the Zohar, the Shekinah is present with them. Neither Britons, Celts, Goths nor Saxons felt any need to dethrone the Divine Feminine, for they simply identified their own great Goddess with the Virgin Mary, or the Sophia of the Greeks, or the Shekinah of the Hebrews.

The Knights Templar named their Lodges after the Virgin Mary; while in civilian life, the troubadours revered the Lady of the

Castle as being made in Mary's image and likeness, even as all mankind is ideally made in the image and likeness of God. And as the monk looked upon his Superior as the representative of Christ, so the knight, fighting the battles of the world, looked upon the Lady as the representative of Mary.

Each knight pledged his devotion to some particular Lady who, by convention, was beautiful, pure and good, as well as wise, and capable of conducting the defense of her castle if the Lord were away. The knight wore his Lady's favor—her colors—on his sleeve or attached to his shield in the jousts and tournaments.

The tournaments were war games which were engaged in by companies of knights. These knights still held to the old teaching of the sanctity of the body as the temple in which the human spirit dwelt as a god, and the tests of athletic and military skill were in the nature of a sacred exercise. At these jousts and tournaments the Ladies were enthusiastic spectators, and were oftentimes chosen as judges to decide the victor, for they had been thoroughly drilled in all the rules and regulations governing tournaments—an important part of the education of every gently-reared lady!

We shall endeavor to lift the beautiful veil of symbology which conceals the deep inner spiritual truths concerned in the careers of King Arthur and his knights. As previously stated, Arthur came as a great Master Teacher, and his Court was in every sense a Mystery School founded in the Name of Christ. The episodes described in the "Idylls" of these knights, and including the trials which came to Arthur himself, portray the experiences which life itself metes out to those who set their feet upon the Path of Discipleship.

The experiences of each Knight are closely bound up with those of his Lady. The Lady typifies the feminine or heart principle within the human spirit, which is allied with the emotional nature. Through the emotions the neophyte meets his most subtle tests and temptations, for it is difficult to detach oneself from intense feeling. It is this feminine principle that, so long as the carnal remains alive in man, leads to perdiction. It is the same feminine principle which, when the carnal man has been lifted up and transformed into spiritual power, leads into Paradise.

Geraint and Enid: The Way of Transmutation

It was King Arthur's custom to celebrate the high holy days with special festivities. Among these holy days the Easter festival stood highest and holiest, and it was on Good Friday that the dove descended to renew the power and mystery of the Holy Grail for another year in the Castle of Carbonek. Arthur's Table Round was the outward reflection of the Table of the Grail, its secular representative so to speak; and in the sacred hour when the dove descended to the Grail, in that same hour the mystic rose in, or above, the center of the Round Table would glow and become luminous with a light that was whiter than snow and brilliant as the sun. Not every eye beheld this transformation, but to some the vision was given, and the story of the flaming white rose passed from mouth to ear among the knights of the inner circle. The white rose is symbolic of the complete transmutation of all that is human into the divine; and this is the highest meaning of Good Friday.

The Feast of Pentecost, which fell in midsummer, was often celebrated with a brilliant tournament, for it was on the Day of Pentecost that Arthur first gathered his knights about his Table, and each year on the same holy day the knights renewed their oaths. It was on the Day of Pentecost, again, that Galahad first came to Arthur's Court, and it was on Pentecost that Galahad was born.

Christmas and Twelfth Night were also occasions for great celebrations; and it was on the Feast of Twelfth Night that Arthur received his kingly Initiation. These midwinter Feasts are complementary to the midsummer Feast of Pentecost; while the Feast of St. Michael (Michaelmas) is complementary to the Eastertide.

It is to be noted that the fires of Pentecost—such as descended upon the disciples after Christ's Ascension—are not the same as those powers which reside in the Holy Grail. The Pentecostal flames pertain to the downpouring Fire which is the Father; whereas the power of the Grail belongs to the Christ Mystery, in which the heart becomes an organ of divine illumination under the control of the will. In the Kabbala the secret of Pentecost is figured in the flaming Chariot of Elijah, who also was able to bring down the fires of heaven to consume the sacrifices placed upon the altar.

It was in the summer season at Caerleon on Usk, Arthur holding court there, that the noble Geraint, oversleeping himself on a morning when Arthur and his knights had gone to hunt a white hart in the forest, rode out in his gay attire, but without arms or armor, to a certain place where he might watch the hunt pass. There he found Queen Guinevere and one of her maidens, who invited him to stay with them to watch the hunt. "For on this knoll, if anywhere," she said, "there is good chance that we shall hear the hounds: here often they break covert at our feet."

While they listened for the distant hunt, there passed slowly by on the road below a knight, lady and dwarf; and since the knight's vizor was up, and Guinevere saw that he was a stranger to Arthur's court, she sent her maiden to inquire of the dwarf who his master might be. The dwarf struck at the maiden with his whip, and Geraint therefore went in her place to ask. Receiving the same treatment, he was forced to retreat with a gash in his cheek. Returning to the Queen, Geraint said that he would avenge the insult done to her through her maid, and also to himself, and rode away hoping to find arms so that he might engage the strange knight in battle, having also promised the Queen that if he were one day to wed he would bring his loved one to Camelot where the Queen would "clothe her with bridals like the sun," even if she were a beggar from the field.

Geraint followed the knight and his companions to a little town in a long valley, where on one side of the valley was a new castle, white from the mason's hand, while on the other was a broken down, and neglected and scarcely habitable ruin. He rode down the street asking for arms, but though the smiths were busy turning out all varieties of armor and arms they refused to part with any, saying that all were needed for a tournament to be held on the morrow. One suggested, however, that perhaps Earl Yniol could provide him with what he needed. Geraint rode across the bridge to the old castle, and was there greeted by Earl Yniol, his wife and his beautiful young daughter Enid, whose voice he had heard in the courtyard as she sang within the castle. Instantly he loved her, saying within himself, "Here by God's grace is the one voice for me."

Tennyson creates, or recreates, a lyric for Enid's song which challenged the wheel of fortune, in which the words, "for man is man and master of his fate," establish the keynote of the story.

Turn, turn thy wheel above the staring crowd;
Thy wheel and thou are shadows in the cloud;
Thy wheel and thee we neither love nor hate.

Such was Geraint's introduction to a maiden as bright and brave of spirit as she was pure and lovely of body.

Geraint learned that Earl Yniol had been deprived of all his wealth, except for this poor castle in which he lives, by the arrogant young knight whom Geraint had followed to the town, the young knight being his nephew, and he was told of the conditions governing the tournament to be held the next day. Geraint immediately offered to fight as champion for Earl Yniol and Enid, and having received rusted and unused armor from the Earl, he appeared in the tourney against Yniol's nephew, Edryn, son of Nudd. Geraint was victor and sent Edryn to Arthur's Court; then, mindful of his promise to the Queen, he insisted that Enid should ride with him to the Court, dressed only in her faded silk dress, so that Guinevere could clothe her for her wedding. So nobly did Guinevere hold to her promise that Enid was second only to the Queen herself in the glory of her attire, as she was also in the grace and loveliness of her person.

Geraint's adoration of his bride was plain to all. He took joy in beholding her arrayed in costly garments and decked with rare jewels, having eyes for no one and for nothing else.

But already the shadow of Lancelot's illicit love for Guinevere had begun to fall upon the Court and the Round Table, and Geraint, fearing Enid's close companionship with the Queen might be to her hurt, asked Arthur's permission to retire to his own estates, on plea of urgent necessity. There he centered his entire attention, his life's interest, in Enid. He forgot his oath of knighthood and his vow of allegiance to the King's service, living for love alone.

Enid was well named "the good," as well as "the fair." She wept bitterly at this state of affairs saying, "I alone am the cause of his dereliction." Weeping and murmuring above him as he slept by her side, her tears falling upon his chest, Enid failed to observe that Geraint had awakened and, listening with closed eyes, heard her say: "O me, I fear that I am no true wife." These words he took to mean that she had been untrue to their wedded love, "weeping for some gay knight in Arthur's hall."

Wrathfully, then, he commanded her to clothe herself in old garments and go with him into the wilderness. She found, where she had tenderly laid it away, the old silken dress she had first worn to Arthur's Court at Caerleon, and attired in this, with gray veil and mantle, rode with her lord, keeping silence, for he had forbidden her to speak.

Sunk in despair and gloom, riding with head bent, Geraint was unaware of three bandits hiding behind a great rock, but Enid saw them, as she was now riding a little ahead, and determined to speak, to warn him of the ambush. Geraint conquered the three bandits, tied their armor on the backs of their three horses and gave the bridle-reins into Enid's hands and directed her to drive and control them, which she did. This happened yet again, so that Enid was driving twice three horses.

There are three distinct steps or stages upon the Way of Attainment. These are generally termed Probationership, Discipleship and Mastership. The horse symbolizes the animalistic nature or "animal soul" and must always be strictly controlled by the feminine or Love power. The threefold battle with the bandits, twice repeated, all of whom are overcome, signifies the overcoming of the lower ambitions and aims which were formerly in the saddle, and their replacement by spiritual objectives in the first two stages mentioned. Geraint, the spiritualized Will, or power-aspect of the ego, warred and overcame; Enid, the Love power and spiritualized understanding, controlled and directed.

There is an important lesson to be learned here, the lesson of discrimination, which every aspirant must learn and in which he is tested over and over again. Geraint had forbidden Enid to speak to him, yet out of her loyalty and love she disobeyed him three times. Similarly the neophyte must determine for himself the right course to pursue in any and every circumstance. He must decide what is the right thing to think, say and do, and then, even though an angel of light urge him otherwise, he must act on his own best understanding. There is absolutely nothing more important to the spiritual life than the ability to discriminate between the good and the bad, the greater good and the lesser good, and to have the courage to carry out the action which conscience then dictates at whatever cost to oneself.

After the trials with the bandits, Geraint and Enid arrived at last before the gates of a great castle in the wilderness. Here Geraint was challenged by a giant whom he must meet in combat. This giant represents what is called in modern occultism "The Dweller on the Threshold," although it is known by other names in myth and legend. This figure is symbolic of the accumulated karma of evil from present and past incarnations. Before the disciple can function at will in the soul world, he must be able to undertake the work of transmuting the essence of past evil which still lingers within his inner being below the threshold of awareness, but it often assumes a symbolical form which the disciple must interpret and understand and promise to redeem. Often the Dweller comes to him under the likeness of a great brooding etheric form which bars his way into the higher soul realms. When the specter is fearlessly confronted and its redemption promised, it vanishes, and the triumphant disciple advances into the Degree of Mastership. His joyous liberation into the inner realms has been accomplished.

It was during this battle with the giant of the castle in the wilderness that Geraint realized Enid's faithfulness and utterly self-sacrificing love; for he was left as one dead, and lying so, heard her conversation with the wild bandit knights in the hall. At last, when the giant earl raised his hand to Enid and slapped her cheek so that she cried out bitterly with pain and humiliation, Geraint could bear no more. He leaped to his feet, seized his sword which lay beside him in the hollow shield, and with a blow severed the brute head from the body. After this they rode together reconciled to Arthur's Hall, where he undertook once more the responsibilities laid upon him by the King, with Enid ever beside him to encourage and advise.

Thereafter Geraint kept the King's justice so surely, yet so compassionately, that the people named him "the Great Prince," and his lady they gratefully called "Enid the Good."

Many lifetimes are necessary to the attainment of the powers of the Initiate. Sometimes the ego's development demands a life in which domestic felicity and companionship are the core of existence. All this is good and noble, but in its very goodness lies a subtle temptation. When the disciple has once dedicated himself to the impersonal life of the Way of Initiation, never again can the limited and limiting personal desires be allowed to take precedence. Human love and companionship may become the central focus of the life, but they can never be made its circumference.

Pelleas and Ettarre

Through the gates of Camelot there came a youth, Pelleas. The fragrance of the fields and the sunshine came with him. "Make me a knight, O Sir King, for I know all the vows of knighthood—and I love!"

Arthur loved this young idealist "whose face shone like a priest of old across the flame of sacrifice kindled by fire from heaven, so glad was he," and instructed Sir Lancelot to guard the ardent youth in his first quest, lest harm befall him.

So together Lancelot and Pelleas set out upon the quest, and in due course came upon a bevy of beautiful maidens, clad in glorious garments, who had lost their way. Ettarre, the fairest, besought Pelleas to guide them to the King and promised that if he were victor in tomorrow's tournament she would be his lady and wear his crown of gold. On the morrow Pelleas won the sword of the victor and placed the circlet of gold upon her head. Then he said: "I am content to see thy face but once a day. I have sworn my vows and thou hast given thy promise. When thou hast seen me strained and sifted to the utmost, thou wilt yield me thy love and know me for thy knight." He then went forth upon his duties and adventures, yet his heart and his mind yearned for Ettare and he took thought for her welfare.

Now it happened that Gawain, the knight who was known as

the light of love, passed that way and offered to visit Ettarre at the castle on Pelleas' behalf, saying that he would return in three days "with golden news." When he did not return, Pelleas went in and found Ettarre sleeping in the arms of Gawain, in a lovely garden of roses, the circlet of gold upon her head. Pelleas turned sadly away, scarcely able to contain himself at the sight of his false friend and false love.

We understand at this point that as in the story of Geraint and Enid we found an object lesson concerning the temptations abiding in conjugal faith and felicity, we have here the opposite—the trial of sorrow and suffering through false love and treachery.

Pelleas' first impulse was the base one to destroy the guilty lovers. But by this time he had passed far beyond the stage where such baseness had power over his soul. He remembered his sacred vow of knighthood, which was centered in the spirit of fellowship and brotherhood. That holy vow must rule all lesser interests. His life was not his own, but had been dedicated to the service of all that lives. Now his heart's agony was overcome in the spirit of compassion. He laid his sword gently across their breasts as they slept, a mute sign of his presence and still more of his forgiveness, and left them still asleep.

Sometimes the most important lesson of life must be learned in sorrow. True indeed are the wise words of Mabel Collins: "Before the feet can stand in the presence of the Master they must be washed in the blood of the heart."

Pelleas had reached the place on the Path where he was able to transmute hate into love and to know only forgiveness for those who had wronged him. This high consummation earned him the help of the Three Queens who were Arthur's teachers and who bore the symbolic names of Faith, Hope and Love.

The keynote of Ettarre is given in her own words: "Whoever loves me must have a touch of earth."

Gareth and Lynette

Gareth, the son of Lot and Bellicent, desired to become a knight at King Arthur's Court. His mother sought to dissuade him, offering him castles, estates and a beautiful bride in his domain.

The youth cried reproachfully: "Oh, Mother, how can you keep me here! For shame! I am a man grown, and a man's work must I do."

On one condition only would she let him go: "Prince, go disguised to Arthur's hall, and hire thyself to serve meats and drinks among the scullions and kitchen knaves." Gareth said: "The thrall in person may be free in soul. I will go."

Attended by two servants who had been with him since birth, he set forth. At last they saw Camelot in the distance, a crown of spires upon a noble hill, which flashed in the sun like a fairy castle, now disappearing in mists, and now gleaming clear and bright, so that the two servants were afraid and declared that this could be no real city, but only a glamor-born dream, a city of enchantment built by fairy kings. The King himself is a changeling, the one servant protests, according to tales he has heard, who drove the heathen from the land by sorcery, with Merlin's aid!

Gareth answered them with laughter, saying that he had enough glamor in his blood—glamor of youth, of hope, of noble lineage—to plunge old Merlin in the Arabian sea; and so drove them forward until they neared the great gates of the city.

The gates were decorated with sculptures representative of the various great events of Arthur's life: the Lady of the Lake, who seemed to uphold the gate; the Three Queens of Faerie who had brought Arthur into the world (and who would help him in his need) and many devices so cunningly inter-worked that as the eye wandered among them it grew 'zzy, and the figures seemed to be alive.

And as they stood before the great gates in amaze, a blast of music issued from the city, and out from under the gate came an ancient man, long-bearded, saying, "Who be ye, my sons?" and Gareth replied, "We be tillers of the soil who have come to see the glories of the King."

The aged one was not deceived; he knew Gareth very well, for he was a seer and a wise man, and he answered the youth's inquiries with a discourse that was only half in jest: "Truly, as thou sayeth, a fairy king and fairy queen have built the city, son; they came from out a sacred mountain cleft toward the sunrise, each with harp in hand, and built it to the music of their harps. . . There is nothing in it as it seems, saving the King; though some there be that hold the King a shadow and the city real. . . For an ye heard a music, like enow they are building still, seeing the city is built to music, therefore never built at all, and therefore built forever."

In such manner do subtle temptations accompany the disciple, ofttimes to the very gates of light, where a Wise One meets him and tests him once again, not with lies but with the truth.

Every occultist knows that all form is created in universal substance (ether) by means of sound and that from each created form there emanates its creative keynote. Thus is formed that sublime symphony which sounds through heaven and earth and which is known as the Music of the Spheres. To earth-dulled ears this music is unreal, because it is not heard until the spiritual senses are awakened and attuned to the song of spirit.

Each initiatory School sounds its own keynote. When the aspirant finds the School to which he is attuned, then despite all difficulties and obstructions the gates will open as easily and as beautifully for him as did the gates of King Arthur's castle for Gareth.

Arrived at Arthur's hall the youth beheld with amaze the marvelous sculpturing of it. "Four great zones of sculpture, with many a mystic symbol gird the hall. In the lowest beasts are slaying men. In the second men are slaying beasts. In the third are warriors, perfect men. In the fourth are men with growing wings. And over all one statue in the mold of Arthur with a crown and golden wings aflame, pointing to the northern star. People in far fields at sunrise seeing the gold and flame cry: We have still a King."

Here Tennyson traces the evolutionary progress of mankind from man's beginnings as a small creature, weaker than many others, to his ultimate destiny as the Winged Man, or superman, of the New Age long prophesied by poets and seers. The constellation Aquarius is this Winged Man of the zodiac, and the Aquarian Age is the Utopia so long foreseen by mystics of all faiths. Tennyson was one of the new generation of scientific poets, and in his day the Darwinian concept of evolution was the storm center of religious and philosophical thinking. His own adherence to the Darwinian theory is shown in this poem, as well as a knowledge of astrology.

> *Then into the hall Gareth ascending heard*
> *A voice, the voice of Arthur, and beheld*
> *Far over heads in that long-vaulted hall*
> *The splendor of the presence of the King*
> *Throned. . . (saw) in all the listening eyes*
>
> *Of those tall knights that ranged about the throne*
> *Clear honor shining like the dewy star*
> *Of dawn, and faith in their great King, with pure*
> *Affection, and the light of victory,*
> *And glory gained, and evermore to gain.*

The shields of the knights, all save one, were brightly emblazoned with designs showing what noble deeds had been done. That of Modred, alone, the evil knight, doer of evil deeds, was dark and blank as death. Even so does the human aura reveal the spiritual status of the individual whom it enhaloes with colors and thought forms of various designs.

With unswerving purpose Gareth bound himself in obedience as kitchen knave, to hew wood, to draw water, to help in preparing and serving food, and to perform any other menial task demanded of him; "and wrought all kinds of service with a noble ease."

This is a lesson every aspirant must learn: that it is the spirit in which a task is done that ennobles; for every necessary work is noble in itself if nobly done.

One day there came to Arthur's Court seeking justice the Lady Lynette, who was barred from her castle by four evil knights, named Morning Star, Noon Sun, Evening Star and Night, or Death, the latter of whom wears a helmet mounted with a skull and on his arms a skeleton.

Gareth promptly petitioned the King for permission to be this Lady's champion, for he loved her on sight, and Arthur granted his wish. Thus released from his vow to his mother, Gareth set forth attendant upon Lynette. Lynette, who believed that the King had treated her with disdain, scoffed at the kitchen knave as she deemed him to be, commanding that he keep his distance for she finds his kitchen odors offensive.

At this point in the story of Gareth and Lynette we are taught concerning the subtle test of acquisitiveness, or the love of personal possessions and worldly status. The Lord Christ taught this lesson in the case of the rich young man who came asking, "What shall I do to inherit eternal life?" To which the Master made answer: "Go, sell all that thou hast and give to the poor, and follow me." The rich young man turned sorrowfully away, for he had great possessions; but the youth Gareth willingly submitted himself to outward humiliation in order to win the honors of a good and noble spirit.

Gareth's mother had first played the part of tempter to the young knight when she put in his path the allurements of estates and riches and a beautiful bride, which should be his for renouncing his spiritual aspirations. He passed this test triumphantly, proving himself a truly illumined soul who had grown beyond the love of worldly things.

His second test was that of humility; a high-born knight compelled to serve as kitchen knave, to attend upon the wants of knights with whom he longed to tread the path of truth and light in equal fellowship.

Again he proved his worth, never hesitating, and performing menial duties with a noble grace of soul.

The test of humility usually comes to the aspirant when he has gone so far that he stands upon the very threshold of illumination. Gareth had shown himself to be an advanced soul. He demonstrated this in his meekness under Lynette's rebukes, and again by his noble amiability when, after conquering the Knight of Death and being accepted into her favor as an honored guest, he generously forebore from any illwill against her. Having overcome all things, Gareth at last won all things. This is the supreme initiatory law. One must be willing to renounce all before he can gain all. This is what is meant by the strait and narrow Path, which is found by few.

Gareth could now sing the triumphant soul song of the conqueror over himself: "There is nothing in all the outer world which can hold my good away from me."

Long ago another great soul walked this Path, met and overcame these same temptations, after which he declared: "Greater is he that controlleth himself than he that taketh a city."

When Lynette had come to Arthur asking for a knight champion, she had expected that he would send the brave Lancelot to rid her of the enemy who surrounded her castle. Her indignation knew no bounds when the King chose Gareth as the knight who was to accompany her. She saw him as a kitchen knave; his true nobility was hidden from her scornful eyes. To recognize human worth regardless of appearances was a lesson she had not learned.

When at each of three bends of the river which surrounded her castle this seeming knave overcame one of three bandits, she recognized him for what he was: no knave, but true knight. The three bends of the river are the three stages of the Path of Preparation as described hitherto: Probationership, Discipleship, Mastership. The names of the three bandits guarding the three bends in the river indicate their nature: Morning Star, Noon Sun, Evening Star, one day in the life of man. The last is Night, or Death. And after these four the fifth conquest was that of the Red Knight of the Red Lawns. The colors of the first three knights were those of the primitive rainbow: Blue, Red and Green, of which Lynette sings:

> O trefoil, sparkling on the rainy plain,
> O rainbow with three colors after rain,
> Shine sweetly; thrice my love has smiled on me.

The trefoil was a sacred emblem of Druidism and was carried over into Druidic Christianity as emblem of the Trinity and of that God who is Light and who set His bow in the cloud. Here as in the Zohar, Green is given as a primary color, with yellow omitted; but Black is added in place of white.

The four Knights of Day and Night, together with the fifth, the Red Knight of the Red Lawns (Desire World) represent all of the temptations that come to the soul by way of the senses throughout the life-day in the school of experience. We are shown that the tests which lead to Initiation come in the course of daily

living, in the work of the world in which the neophyte finds
himself stationed by the Lords of Destiny. It is not by isolating
oneself and withdrawing from human contacts that the greatest
strength is attained, but in learning to "live the life" amid the
stress and discord of the world.

When Gareth overcame the first bandit knight, Lynette smiled
upon him and sang joyously, "At last my love has smiled on me."
And with the overcoming of the third, when she invited Gareth to
ride beside her, she sang, "Three times my love has smiled on me."
Side by side they approached the entrance to the castle where
Gareth was confronted by the dark-armored gruesome figure of
the Knight of Death; but riding fearlessly he found Death
suddenly transformed into a beautiful cherub who gave him his
blessing. And the poet adds that the four knights of his story were
simply imitating certain rock-hewn pictures on a cliff nearby, and
from this had drawn name and color of armor, and that the whole
of it was an allegory of the soul's progress from birth to death, and
from ignorance to wisdom.

We have said before that the most precious heritage of Initiation
is the first-hand knowledge that there is no death and that life is
eternal. This Gareth learns when he overcomes the fourth
knight-bandit.

Now, hand in hand, Gareth and Lynette pass through the wide
open portals and enter together into the Castle of Understanding.

Merlin and Vivien

Merlin, the Archdruid of Christ, was famous for his great
wisdom. Men whispered that he was in very truth the architect of
Stonehenge, so ancient he seemed, and said that he knew a magic
taught him by a hermit in the deep woods to whom the curtain
that separates spirit from matter was clear as glass, so that he
could control the elements of nature.

Merlin knew the ancient teachings handed down from the
farthest past-from Lemuria and Atlantis, from Babylon and Egypt,
from Greece and Rome-and summed it up in the sublime wisdom
of Glastonbury. Born of a "human" Christian mother and an
"archdemon" (Druid High Priest) father, his name was said to
signify "serpent babe" or "wondrus one", for he possessed the

wisdom of the serpent without its guile. He was a strange being in whom Celtic magic and Christian mysticism were blended. He was able to read the events of the past and future, and the young knights of King Arthur's Court looked upon him with awe and reverence, going softly in fear of his power and in respect of his vast learning. His somber figure appeared and disappeared miraculously. Tall, brown, lean, and rough of hair, he lived much alone in the great woods and waste places where demoniac spirits drew him.

Tennyson conveys the idea that Merlin was in his dotage when he fell prey to the seduction of the sorceress Vivien; but other tales have it that she was a follower of the old gods who came to Merlin for instruction, as many of the old religion did, combining their own ancient tradition with that of Christ. The Lady of the Lake, who broods over King Arthur's Court throughout the Idylls, is still another of the great teachers of the ancient Druid wisdom who "put on the Christ." It was she who gave to the King his sword Excalibur, a huge crosshilted sword, and was the foster mother of Lancelot. "A mist of incense curled about her and her face was well-nigh hidden in the minister gloom, but there was heard among the holy hymns a voice as of the waters."

But Vivien was "born among the dead." She could not take the step forward which would bring her to Christ and the powers of the Grail. Her parents had fallen in battle against Arthur's hosts, she herself was born from her dying mother on the battlefield, and she lived only for revenge and to destroy, if possible, the knighthood of the Grail. Her mother had died cursing King Arthur and all his Court.

The feminine in man debases or exalts, drags down or lifts up. Vivien came, says the poet, "like a baleful star clothed in grey vapor." She first endeavored to subdue Arthur with her charms, but he was beyond beguilement. Next she turned to the wise Merlin and succeeded in persuading him to take her for a pupil, and he taught her the secrets of his magic, all save one, which he had learned from the ancient hermit in the wood, and which, in other hands, could bring about his undoing.

But the witch Vivien, with her flaming hair and green eyes and her passion for learning, at last won his confidence—through her seductive beauty. Tennyson would have us believe, for he portrays her as a Kundry, a temptress, who had power over the magician's senses as Kundry had over Amfortas. She represents the lure of the old religion. Her power is greatest in the wild dark woods of Brittany, among the elemental forces dedicated to the service of the Black Grail.

One day as Merlin and Vivien walked hand and hand in the wild forest of Broceliande in Brittany, having sailed thither in a little boat, they became weary, and when a sudden thunder storm arose, took shelter under a blossoming hawthorn tree. (Some say a hollow oak.) Merlin laid his head in the maiden's lap and was soon deep in slumber.

Then Vivien arose and, with her wimple, made a ring round about the bush and round about Merlin who slept under it; and she began the enchantment as he himself had taught her. Nine times she made the ring, and nine times she made the enchantment, and then she went and sat down by him and took his head again upon her lap. And when he awoke and looked around him, it seemed to him that he was enclosed in the strongest tower in the world and laid upon a fair bed. Then said he to the maid, "My lady, you have deceived me. Abide with me, for no one hath power to unmake this tower but you alone."

She promised that she would be often with him there, and this covenant she kept. Merlin nevermore left the tower wherein Vivien had enclosed him, but she entered and went out again when she listed.

Merlin typifies the individual who enters the Way of Attainment impelled only by an eager thirst for knowledge. Such an one will devote every available moment to reading and study neglecting all opportunities to give of himself in love and serving for others. Inevitably his narrowness of outlook brings about a one-sided development which can end only in sorrow and disillusionment. Saint Paul refers to the unillumined intellect as "the power of darkness." The aspirant who is working for well-rounded development will for each important occult truth that he learns give of himself anew in loving, self-forgetting service for the betterment of some one of God's creatures. If mind and heart are working equally together, the fate of Merlin will be an impossibility.

It is significant to note that mind occultly correlates with the element of air. Vivien's magic tower in which she encased Merlin was fashioned of air. It was an enchantment of the mind only.

Elaine—Lancelot—Guinevere

The ancient wisdom possessed a glyph which showed the aspirant at a certain stage of development. He stands between two beautiful maidens, one crowned with the leaves of the vine, typifying the lure of the personality, the other crowned with stars, the way of the Spirit. Each aspirant must come to this place of choosing, where he will decide which of the two maidens he will make his own. Nowhere in the Mystery epics is this story of decision more strikingly told than in the story of the young knight Lancelot.

Lancelot came to Arthur's Court when he was about nineteen years of age. Comely and gifted, venturesome and filled with idealistic enthusiasm, he soon was a prime favorite with all the Court, and most of all with King Arthur himself. When the King wished to send an envoy to escort the young princess Guinevere to the castle where she was to become his bride, he chose the handsome Sir Lancelot as his emissary.

When Guinevere saw Lancelot she mistook him for the King and gave him her heart at first sight. Neither Guinevere nor Lancelot ever forgot that wondrous journey which they made together to King Arthur's Court. They travelled through far-stretching meadows fragrant with sheets of waving hyacinth, and on a road beneath great trees filled with singing birds. Before they reached the castle they had pledged their love forever.

Lancelot was known far and wide for his bravery and for his skill in all knightly accomplishments. He was inevitably the hero in every tournament in which he chose to make trail of arms and was greatly admired and sought after by great ladies everywhere. Yet throughout his earlier life he loved Guinevere alone, to the hurt of himself and the whole Court.

Among the many romantic adventures which fell to him was that of the maiden Elaine. It chanced that he was to take part in a famous contest, and he had decided that he would enter the lists incognito, fighting unknown. He therefore journeyed to the castle of Astolat, which was the home of a distinguished knight, Sir Gervaine, who lent him his sword. Sir Gervaine had a daughter named Elaine, who by reason of her purity and beauty was known as the Lily Maid of Astolat. She, like Guinevere, loved Lancelot at first sight, and asked that he wear her colors in the tournament. Lancelot had promised Guinevere that he would never wear any colors save hers, but thinking that this would make his disguise more complete he accepted the young maid's offer and wore her tokens, a handsome red sleeve richly embroidered with rare pearls. Lancelot was again the victor. It happened that Sir Gawain, one of King Arthur's knights, being in the vicinity, attended the tournament and recognized the hero. He carried the story back to King Arthur's Court, and as he described the beautiful maiden whose colors Lancelot had worn, Guinevere was filled with anger and humiliation.

Injured in the tournament, Lancelot was taken back to the castle of Astolat where Elaine nursed him day and night until he recovered. It was then that she told him of her great love, and asked that he might give his in return. Gently but firmly he replied that he could not do this, for his heart was no longer in his own keeping.

When Lancelot had gone away Elaine told her brother that since Lancelot could not love her, she must die; but first she must write a letter to the knight.

When her brother offered to take the letter to Lancelot she declared that this could not be, for she, and she alone, must deliver her message.

I fain would follow Love if that could be,
I needs must follow Death who waits for me.

She bade them send her body in a barge to Camelot: "In her right hand the lily, in her left the letter, all her bright hair streaming down; all the coverlet was cloth of gold, and she in white; her clear-cut features smiling as though she were asleep." And so the barge drifted down to Camelot and came to rest under the Queen's windows.

At this moment Lancelot entered the Queen's chamber. For nine successive years he had taken part in nine tournaments and won them all, the prize in each having been a magnificent diamond, which he had kept to present all together to the Queen, but Guinevere, in jealous rage, rushed to the casement window and cast the diamonds into the river far below. They gleamed like sinking stars as they fell into the water beside the boat on which lay the Lily Maid of Astolat.

Again, this is the story of the choice which must be made between earthly and heavenly love, the love of personality and the love of the spirit and spiritual things. The ordinary person makes the choice that Lancelot made, having no concept of the infinite joy and bliss which attend on the dedication of the life to the things of Spirit. Therefore it is that the Lily Maid must sleep upon the waters of time until the mind of mankind awakens to know the high meaning of life.

The nine diamonds are the glory of the Nine Lesser Mysteries. King Arthur's Court, as we have said, is the continuation of the Mystery School of early Christianity. Since there are but few now, as in the time of Christ, who are ready to receive the profound teachings of Esoteric Christianity, the diamonds of the Mysteries are lost until humanity is sufficiently advanced to recover them.

After the adventure of Astolat the relationship between Guinevere and Lancelot was never again the same. A cloud of doubt and suspicion had drifted between them. Guinevere could not countenance Lancelot's reverence for the Lily Maid, while for Lancelot the Lily Maid's beauty and purity of spirit had awakened his aspiration afresh, and he knew that his illicit love of the Queen would forever prevent him from attaining the Quest of the Grail.

A soft white cloud may appear above the horizon of a clear blue sky and give no portent of evil. Yet, joined by other clouds, the sky is soon overcast and the fury of the storm may devastate the landscape. Even so the little cloud which was the guilty love of Lancelot and Guinevere cast the first shadow upon the glories of King Arthur's Court. Wrongdoing is contagious, and gradually other knights began to respond to the subtle influence of hidden lawlessness which pervaded the Court, until it seemed that they lived for pleasure alone, dead to the call of knightly courtesy. Thus the cycle of dissolution began. The light of the Grail slowly dimmed, and in the last tournament we hear the knights making light of holy things, even to the forgetting of their sacred vow of knighthood.

The man of the world, who lives only from moment to moment, believes that he can live as he likes so long as he is not caught by the law of the land, enjoying the pleasures of the senses; but the esotericist knows that there is a Law of Cause and Effect which governs the entire universe, in the small things as in the great. It manifests in every aspect of the life of every individual and every nation and is nowhere more clearly and plainly stated than in the Bible: "Whatsoever a man sows that shall he also reap."

It would be well if this statement of the cosmic law could be indelibly inscribed upon the soul of every human being in the world, for the time is not far distant when our civilization must face the fruits of its past sowing, keeping the good and casting out the evil in preparation for the New Age.

Sir Lancelot and Guinevere were reconciled, but their love was more troubled than before. Not only had the Queen's jealousy of Elaine come between them, but her power over Lancelot had caused him to fail in the Quest of the Holy Grail; and he could not put from his mind the vision of the spiritual joy he could not win, whose loss he continually mourned.

Jealousy and ambition had grown among the knights of the Round Table, too, as the spirit of fellowship waned. Finally Modred and his brother Agravaine, who had long brewed mischief, denounced the lovers to Arthur and attacked Lancelot in Guinevere's chamber. Lancelot, though unarmed, fought his way to safety, but Guinevere was in the enemy's hands. Arthur's grief, as Malory describes it, seems more for Lancelot than for Guinevere, whose lack of true affection must have been apparent long since. "'Alas, me sore repenteth,' said the King, 'that ever Sir Lancelot should be against me. Now I am sure the noble fellowship of the Round Table is broken forever, for with him will many a noble knight hold.'"

Some say that Arthur condemned his Queen to be burnt at the stake because of her adultery, such being the law of the land; but Lancelot and his friends carried Guinevere to his Castle, Joyous Gard. Arthur beseiged him there, though unwillingly, for he often thought on "the great courtesy that was in Sir Lancelot more than in any other man." And Lancelot lamented: "I have no heart to fight against my Lord Arthur, for ever me seemeth I do not as I ought to do."

At last the Pope commanded Arthur to receive Guinevere back with honor, and Lancelot departed across the sea to France. As Arthur had foreseen, many good knights went with Lancelot, although he besought them to stay with the King, warning them that Modred meant treachery.

Arthur gathered together an army and followed Lancelot to France, spurred on by Gawain whose brothers Lancelot had killed while rescuing Guinevere. This was Modred's opportunity. He seized the kingdom and declared that he would marry Guinevere, whereupon the Queen shut herself in the Tower of London. Arthur then came quickly back to London, but with only a remnant of his knights, for many had fallen in the battles with Lancelot and his hosts. The King won the last battle, but would see Guinevere no more. After Arthur's death, Guinevere entered a nunnery.

Lancelot, hearing in France of Arthur's troubles hastened back to England to help him, only to learn of his death and Guinevere's retreat to a convent. The poignant story is told of Lancelot's farewell visit with Guinevere: "At last he came to a nunnery, and then was Queen Guinevere aware of Sir Lancelot as he walked in the cloister. And when she saw him there she swooned thrice, that all the ladies and gentlewomen had work enough to hold the Queen up. . . When Sir Lancelot was brought to her, then she said to all the ladies: 'Through this man and me hath all this war been wrought, and the death of the most noblest knights of the world; for through our love that we have loved together is my most noble lord slain. . . Therefore, Sir Lancelot, I require of thee and beseech thee heartily, for all the love that ever was betwixt us, that thou never see me more. . .for as well as I have loved thee, mine heart will not serve me to see thee, for through thee and me is the flower of kings and knights destroyed; therefore, Sir Lancelot, go to thy realm, and there take thee a wife, and live with her in joy and bliss. . .' 'Now, sweet madam,' said Sir Lancelot, 'would ye that I return again to my country, and there to wed a lady? Nay, madam, wit ye well that I shall never do. . .but the same destiny that ye have taken ye have taken you to perfection, I must needs take me to perfection, of right. For I take record of God, in you have I had mine earthly joy; and if I had found you now so disposed, I had cast to have had you in mine own realm. . . Wherefore, madam, I pray you kiss me and never no more.' 'Nay,' said the Queen, 'that shall I never do, but abstain you from such words'; and they departed."

Lancelot went his way weeping, and came to a hermitage where he dwelt with Sir Bedivere and Sir Bors and seven other knights of the Round Table, until there came to him a vision in which he saw that Guinevere was dead, and in which he was instructed to take her body and bury it beside King Arthur.

So Lancelot went with his fellows to the nunnery and carried the Queen's body to Glastonbury and laid her with the King. After this, Lancelot "ate but little meat, ne drank, till he was dead." Six weeks after Guinevere's death the hermit dreamed that "he saw the angels heave up Sir Lancelot into heaven," and when he went to Lancelot's cell he found him "stark dead, and he lay as he had smiled." Then Lancelot's companions took him and buried him as he had desired at Joyous Gard, and there Sir Ector de Maris bade him farewell in words that might serve as a lament for all of medieval chivalry:

"Ah Lancelot," he said, "thou wert head of all Christian knights, and now I dare say, thou Sir Lancelot, there thou liest, thou that were never matched of earthly knight's hand. And thou wert the courteousest knight that ever bare shield. And thou wert the truest friend to thy friend that ever bestrode horse. And thou sert the truest lover of a sinful man that ever loved a woman. And thou wert the kindest man that ever struck with sword. And thou were the goodliest person that ever came among press of knights. And thou wert the meekest man and the gentlest that ever ate in hall among ladies. And thou wert the sternest knight to thy mortal foe that ever put spear in the rest."

In the story of Lancelot we have evidence that the trials which overtake the aspirant on the heart path may be more cataclysmic than those of the aspirant on the head path, such as Merlin. For it was not Merlin's failure that caused the disruption of King Arthur's Court; it was the defections of those like Lancelot, who were following the path of the heart who were largely responsible for bringing about the destruction of the Order of the Round Table and the dispersion of those knights whom Tennyson has described as "that glorious company, the flower of all men."

As the modern aspirant ponders on these things, it is well for him to take courage from the words of the great Christian Initiate Saint Paul, who was familiar with all the subtle tests and trials which beset both head and heart, and of which he continually warned. For if he described the mortal intellect as "the power of darkness," he pointed to the remedy when he said, "Have that mind in you which was also in Christ Jesus, that ye may be transformed by the renewing of your mind."

Of the even more subtle tests which beset those on the heart path, he instructed his pupils that they must learn to "put on the whole armor of God." In other words, they must surround themselves at all times with All-Good, thinking only Christed thoughts, speaking only Christed words, and performing only Christed deeds. Finally, and perhaps this is his most important word of instruction, applying equally to aspirants on both head and heart paths, he said, "Pray without ceasing."

PART III

THE CYCLE OF DISSOLUTION

Chapter VI

THE QUEST OF THE HOLY GRAIL

The Holy Grail, which had disappeared from the outer world before the coming of Arthur, reappeared in a vision to a nun, the sister of Sir Percival:

> *If ever holy maid*
> *With knees of adoration wore the stone,*
> *A holy maid. . . .*
> *And he to whom she told her sins, or what*
> *Her all but utter whiteness, held for sin,*
> *A man wellnigh a hundred winters old,*
> *Spake often with her of the Holy Grail,*
> *A legend handed down through five or six,*
> *And each of these a hundred winters old,*
> *From our Lord's time.*

Hearing, even in her cloistered cell, of the evils which were rife in Arthur's Court, this holy nun gave herself over to the continual prayer and fasting, until she was as transparent as a wraith, and it seemed that the sun shone and the wind blew through her, and her eyes were like brilliant lamps in the pure palor of her face. To her, in her cell, the Grail came, descending in a beam of light, "rose-red with beatings in it," attended by angelic music; and the walls of her white cell were shimmering in its crimson glow, until at last it was wafted away from her sight, and the celestial music went with it.

After this came a year of miracle, in which Galahad came to Arthur's Court and was knighted, and the Grail appeared in the hall, but under a veil, so that none but Galahad saw it clear.

Then inflamed by the vision, impetuous Sir Gawain rose to his feet and pledged himself to go in search of the Grail for twelve months and a day and not to return until he had seen it uncovered, and the other knights followed suit. But Arthur protested, knowing that most of these men were not fitted for the Quest and that their defection from their duties as governors and protectors of the realm must inevitably lead to the downfall of his kingdom. Yet all took the pledge to return one year and a day later to Arthur's hall.

Sir Gawain was known throughout King Arthur's realm as the light of love. His fancy roamed from one fair maid to another, as the butterfly in the garden flits from flower to flower. Filled with high enthusiasm he started along the shining Path which would lead to the Grail when his attention was distracted by the sight of a group of beautiful maidens dancing in a pavilion, and he tarried to sport with them; but suddenly they dissolved into nothingness, and he was left alone. Disconsolately he turned to resume his journey, only to find that the Path also had vanished, and a Voice said in his heart, "The Quest is not for you."

Events in the life of Gawain typify obstacles which all too often impede the progress of the aspiring. Although idealistic in temperament, with high concepts of devotion and duty, he was yet lacking in the perseverence and continuity of purpose necessary to bring his idealism to fruitage.

Sir Bors was another who set out on the Quest of the Holy Grail. After he had travelled some way along the shining Path, he came upon a great tree laden with golden fruit. He, like Gawain, left the Path, thinking to enjoy the tempting fruit, but when he laid his hands upon it, it turned into ashes. Chagrined and humiliated he returned whence he had come, but the Path was no longer there. He, too, heard the Voice say, "The Quest is not for you."

Yet Sir Bors, together with Percival, ultimately achieved the rare privilege of traveling on Solomon's Ship to the Spiritual City of Sarras, accompanying Galahad when he sailed thither with the Holy Cup. Tennyson says of Sir Bors (it is Sir Percival speaking):

> One night my pathway swerving east, I saw
> The pelican on the casque of our Sir Bors:

and we are reminded that Sir Bors, when questing for the Grail, came upon a dead tree in a forest, in which was perched a pelican who was tearing her breast with her bill to feed her starving young

ones. The pelican is a well known Rosicrucian symbol, and here
we have a hint of the role which Sir Bors plays in the epic of the
Holy Grail.

Tennyson continues:

> *And then, with small adventure met,*
> *Rode to the lonest tract of all the realm,*
> *And found a people there among their crags,*
> *Our race and blood, a remnant that were left*
> *Paynim amid their circles, and the stones*
> *They pitch up straight to heaven; and their wise men*
> *Were strong in the old magic which can trace*
> *The wandering of the stars, and scoffed at him*
> *And this high quest as at a simple thing,*
> *Told him he followed—almost Arthur's words—*
> *A mocking fire: "What other fire than he*
> *Whereby the blood beats, and the blossom blows,*
> *And the sea rolls, and all the world is warmed?"*

That is, these were star and sun worshippers—Druids who were
called "Culdees"—who did not accept the Christ, and they threw
Sir Bors in prison; yet was he not without comfort, for a stone fell
away from the roof of his dungeon:

> *Then came a night*
> *Still as the day was loud, and thro' the gap*
> *The seven clear stars of Arthur's Table Round—*
> *For, brother, so one night, because they roll*
> *Thro' such a round in heaven, we named the stars,*
> *Rejoicing in ourselves and in the King—*
> *And these, like bright eyes of familiar friends,*
> *In on him shone: "And then to me, to me,"*
> *Said good Sir Bors, "beyond all hopes of mine*
> *Who scarce had prayed or asked it for myself—*
> *Across the seven clear stars—O grace to me!—*
> *In color like the fingers of a hand*
> *Before a burning taper, the sweet Grail*
> *Glided and past, and close upon it pealed*
> *A sharp quick thunder."*

Afterward Sir Bors was released from the dungeon by a maid

who was secretly of the Christian faith; and later met with Galahad and Percival aboard the "Ship of Faith" which would take the Grail to Sarras. Sir Bors returned from Sarras, for his work lay in the world, not in the far "Spiritual City." Percival, however, who on the Quest found life to be nought but disillusionment, retired to a monastery, renouncing forever the woman whom he had loved from childhood.

The Bible says that the love of money is the root of all evil; yet we understand by this not that money in itself is evil but only the excessive love of money, or its misuse, is evil. To be the steward of great wealth, and to use it for the betterment of mankind is sometimes the rare privilege given to an advanced soul. However, like most men, Sir Bors at first experienced the lure of gold and power, and this threatened for a time to outweigh the Quest of Holiness. The *lesson of discrimination* having been learned, Sir Bors continued on his Quest. Here we may find a hint of the alchemical Quest of the Rosicrucian, which transmutes the base metals into gold.

Sir Lancelot, in all good faith, had long been following the Shining Way. His spirit's ardor flamed high, and sometimes he would hear the chanting of the angels who guarded the Grail, and sometimes he sensed the celestial incense which floated about it.

It befell upon a certain midnight when the moon shone clear that Lancelot, driven mad by grief and longing and the conflict in his soul, sailing in his ship, came to a certain place where he saw, high upon a rocky shore, a fair castle of which the postern gate stood open against the sea, and it was guarded by two lions; and he heard a Voice which spoke in his ear, saying, "Leave now thy ship and go within the castle and thou shalt see a part of thy desire."

Then he armed himself and went up to the lion-guarded gate and there drew out his sword and made as if to slay the lions, but a dwarf came out and fiercely attacked him, smiting him so sorely upon the arm that he let fall his sword; and then once again he heard the Voice: "Oh man of evil faith and poor belief, wherefore trusteth thou thine arms before thy Maker?" At these words Lancelot put up his sword and signed himself upon the forehead;

and when the two lions beheld that sign they held back, and he passed safely into the great empty hall. Then hearing the high sweet sound of a voice singing, he followed the sound through the castle until he came to the easternmost tower, and he climbed as it seemed a thousand steps to the top of that tower, and there he found a chamber with the door close shut, and with all his strength he was not able to open it. Yet through the door he saw gleaming lights and heard the voice singing sweetly, as if it were an angel, "Joy and honor to the Father of Heaven and to the Holy Vessel of the Grail!" And he knelt reverently at the door's threshold, for well he understood what was within.

Yet though he could not force the door, it opened of a sudden, not as with hands but of its own accord, and thereout came a great splendor of light, "as if all the torches of the world had been alight together." But when he would have stepped over the threshold, the Voice forbade, and he drew back his foot and stood gazing in through the open door. He saw there a table of silver and upon it the holy vessel covered with red samite, and there were choirs of angels round about holding burning candles in their hands, and he saw a cross, and all the ornaments of the altar.

Then a priest before the altar offered up Mass, and taking the covered Cup he would have raised it up, but it seemed heavy, and he seemed to sink under its weight. Seeing which, Sir Lancelot cried, "O Father, take it not for sin that I go in to help the priest, who hath much need thereof." So saying he went in, but as he approached the table there came toward him a breath of fire which smote him to the ground, and he lay in a deep swoon, yet felt hands take him up and lay him down outside the chapel door where he continued to lie throughout the night, and was there found senseless on the morrow. Unconscious he was borne to an inner chamber to rest, and he slept, living, but without movement, for twenty-four days and nights, and on the twenty-fifth day he opened his eyes, and said to those standing near, "Why have ye waked me? for I have seen wonders that no tongue can tell, and more than any heart can think." Then he asked where he was, and they said, "In the castle of Carbonek," and he commanded them to tell their lord King Pelles, that he was Sir Lancelot, which they did.

King Pelles was overjoyed to have this great and honorable knight in his house and urged him to abide for as long as he needed until he was wholly well, but Sir Lancelot said: "I know well that I have now seen as much as mine eyes may behold of the Holy Grail; wherefore I will return to my own country."

Forever afterward, so long as he lived, Lancelot thought of these wonders in an agony of longing, falling upon his knees and weeping bitter tears of contrition for the sins which had caused him to see the Grail through a veil only; yet lesser knights fared worse and saw less, though he, of tender conscience and noble spirit, wept his spirit's loss.

For the dust of earth had blinded his eyes. In deep grief Lancelot and those other knights who had failed in the Quest turned away, remembering the sad words of the King when he had sought to dissuade them from the adventure of the Grail: "You are following wandering fires. The Quest is not for you."

It was the failure of his knights to live steadfastly true to their vows that brought about the final wars in which King Arthur suffered a fatal wound. All great World Teachers have met with a similar reception. They come unto their own, but their own receive them not.

When the twelve months were gone, then on the next day after the knights assembled once again in Arthur's hall, only a remnant of the glorious company which had set out with high hopes on the Quest.

Tennyson's words, spoken by the sad-faced King, are memorable:

> But if indeed there came a sign from heaven
> Blessed are Bors, Lancelot, and Percivale,
> For these have seen according to their sight.
> And spake I not too truly, O my knights?
> Was I too dark a prophet when I said
> To those who went upon the Holy Quest
> That most of them would follow wandering fires,
> Lost in the quagmire? lost to me and gone,
> And left me gazing at a barren board,
> And a lean Order—scarce returned a tithe—

And out of those to whom the vision came
My greatest hardly will believe he saw.
Another hath beheld it afar off,
And leaving human wrongs to right themselves
Cares but to pass into the silent life.
And one hath had the vision face to face,
And now his chair desires him here in vain,
However they may crown him otherwhere.

And some among you held that if the King
Had seen the sight he would have sworn the vow.
Not easily, seeing that the King must guard
That which he rules. . .
Let visions of the night or of the day
Come as they will; and many a time they come,
Until this earth he walks on seems not earth,
This light that strikes his eyeballs is not light,
This air that smites his forehead is not air,
But vision—his very hand and foot—
In moments when he feels he cannot die,
And knows himself no vision to himself,
Nor the high God a vision, nor that One
Who rose again. Ye have seen what ye have seen.

Chapter VII

THE LAST TOURNAMENT

In his portrayal of the Last Tournament Tennyson chants the Swan Song of a decadent chivalry.

The prize of this tourney was to be a circlet of rubies which had belonged to Guinevere's adopted child who had died in infancy, and she could no longer bear the sad memories which the rubies brought to her mind. She therefore gave the circlet to the King, suggesting that these be the prize in the tourney—

> *rosier luck will go*
> *With these rich jewels, seeing that they came*
> *Not from the skeleton of a brother-slayer*
> *But the sweet body of a maiden babe.*

The tournament was called, therefore, the Tournament of the Dead Innocence, to the ironic delight of the knights.

Arthur knew well that evil was aboard in his court, and that the courtly love between Lancelot and Guinevere was an open jest, and he hinted as much to Lancelot when, greatly to the latter's dismay, he appointed him to judge the tournament and award the prize. Lancelot spent the night tossing miserably, unable to sleep, for he loved the King and yet could not give up the Queen.

> *But when the morning of the tournament,*
> *By these in earnest those in mockery called,*
> *The Tournament of the Dead Innocence,*
> *Brake off with a wet wind blowing, Lancelot,*
> *Round whose sick head all night, like birds of prey,*
> *The words of Arthur flying shrieked, arose,*
> *And down a streetway hung with folds of pure*
> *White samite, and by fountains running wine,*
> *Where children sat in white with cups of gold,*
> *Moved to the lists, and there, with slow sad steps*
> *Ascending, filled his (Arthur's) double-dragoned chair.*

Forced by the King to judge the tourney, Lancelot sits in the dragon chair in deep agony of soul, avoiding the bright eyes of the brilliantly clad ladies, paying scant attention to the fray raging below him, allowing foul play without word of rebuke, beheld the laughing, irreverent, but formidable, Sir Tristram of the Woods wearing a holly-spray for crest, strike his opponents down with light-hearted ease, until he muttered to himself: "Craven crests! O shame! What faith have these in whom they sware to love? The glory of the Round Table is no more."

So Tristram won the rubies and received them from Lancelot's hands, who said bitterly, "Hast thou won? Art thou the purest, brother? See, the hand wherewith thou takest this is red!" and Tristram replied angrily: "Wherefore toss me this like a dry bone cast to some hungry hound?. . . Be happy in thy fair Queen as I in mine." For Tristram's fateful love for Isolt was as publicly known as Lancelot's for Guinevere.

Then boldly, without shame, Tristram made his horse caracole around the gallery where the ladies sat, bowed his homage and said: "Behold, this day my Queen of Beauty is not here!" And many were offended by this frank mention of his illicit love, and many murmured, "All courtesy is dead;" and one said, "The glory of our Round Table is no more."

Then the thick rain fell, plume drooped and mantle clung, and the wan day went glooming down in wet and weariness, and a swarthy lady shrilled: "Praise the patient saints, our one white day of Innocence hath past, though somewhat draggled at the skirt. So be it. The snowdrop only, flowering through the year, would make the world as blank as wintertide. Come, let us gladden their sad eyes, our Queen's and Lancelot's, at this night's solemnity with all the kindlier colors of the field."

So dame and damsel glittered at the feast variously gay, clad in all the bright bold colors of the summer, full and ripe and with nothing of delicacy or innocence. Then the feast became so loud and boisterous that the Queen, disapproving, angry at Tristram and the lawless jesting, broke up the feast and departed slowly to her bower.

And Arthur's jester, Dragonet, skipping about the hall, makes bitter jests to Tristram who has asked, in response to a quip, "Is the King thy brother fool?", replying: "Ay, my brother fool, the king of fools! Conceits himself as God that he can make figs out of thistles, silk from bristles, milk from burning spurge, honey from hornet-crumbs, and men from beasts—long live the king of fools!" Then down the city Dragonet danced away; and slowly through the woods Tristram rode to Lyonesse, bearing the ruby-chain as a gift for Isolt, and received his death at the hand of her husband King Mark.

It was this famous love story of the knight Tristram and Isolt, the wife of King Mark of Brittany, on which Richard Wagner built his glorious music-drama, Tristram and Isolde.

> *That night came Arthur home, and while he climbed*
> *All in a death-dumb autumn-dripping gloom*
> *The stairway to the hall, and looked and saw*
> *The great Queen's bower was dark—about his feet*
> *A voice clung sobbing till he questioned it,*
> *"What art thou?" and the voice about his feet*
> *Sent up an answer, sobbing, "I am thy fool,*
> *And I shall never make thee smile again."*

The bower was dark indeed, for Guinevere had fled to the nuns at Almesbury. There she asked protection, saying, "Mine enemies pursue me, Oh peaceful Sisterhood. Yield me sanctuary, nor ask her name to whom ye yield it." Once more her beauty, grace and power worked as a charm, upon these saintly women as on all others, and the stately Queen abode for many weeks among the nuns. There pondering on the past, she remembers how when she first saw the King she thought him cold, high, self-contained and passionless, "not like him, not like my Lancelot." Then one night the light of the Dragonship blazed amid the gloom, and there were cries: "The King comes!"

> *She sat stiff-stricken, listening; but when armed feet*
> *Through the long gallery from the outer doors*
> *Rang coming, prone from off her seat she fell.*
> *And grovelled with her face against the floor.*
>
> *There with her milk-white arms and shadowy hair*
> *She made her face a darkness from the King,*

> *And in the darkness heard his armed feet*
> *Pause by her; then came silence, then a voice,*
> *Monotonous and hollow like a ghost's!*

An ancient bard had once prophesied concerning Arthur:

> *. . . That his grave should be a mystery*
> *From all men, like his birth; and could he find*
> *A woman in her womanhood as great*
> *As he was in his manhood, then, he sang,*
> *The twain together well might change the world.*

This was not to be. Now the King speaks:

> *Howbeit I know, if ancient prophecies*
> *Have erred not, that I march to meet my doom.*
> *Thou hast not made my life so sweet to me*
> *That I the King should greatly care to live;*
> *For thou hast spoilt the purpose of my life.*

$$O \quad O \quad O \quad O$$

> *But I was first of all the kings who drew*
> *The knighthood-errant of this realm and all*
> *The realms together under me, their Head,*
> *In that fair Order of my Table Round,*
> *A glorious company, the flower of men,*
> *To serve as model for the mighty world*
> *And be the fair beginning of a time.*
> *I made them lay their hands in mine and swear*
> *To reverence the King as if he were*
> *Their conscience, and their conscience as their King,*
> *To break the heathen and uphold the Christ,*
> *To ride abroad redressing human wrongs,*
> *To speak no slander, no, nor listen to it,*
> *To honor his own word as if his God's,*
> *To lead sweet lives in purest chastity,*
> *To love one maiden only, cleave to her,*
> *And worship her by years of noble deeds*
> *Until they won her; for indeed I knew*
> *Of no more subtle master under heaven*
> *Than is the maiden passion of a maid*
> *Not only to keep down the base in man*

But teach him high thought, and amiable words,
And courtliness, and the desire of fame,
And love of truth, and all that makes a man.
Then came thy shameful sin with Lancelot,
Then came the sin of Tristram and Isolt;
Then others, following these my mightiest knights.

In some versions of the legend, as we have shown, Arthur condemns his Queen to the stake; she is rescued by Lancelot and taken to France; the pope commands Arthur to receive her back with honor, which he consents to do; Guinevere enters a nunnery; and meanwhile Modred has led a rebellion against Arthur, in which Arthur is slain and disappears, and Lancelot and Guinevere die in their respective sacred retreats.

Tennyson, however, shows only, of all this, King Arthur forgiving his Queen. "Lo, I forgive thee, as Eternal God forgives! do thou for thine own soul the rest." Then he leaves her, while she is yet silent and unable to speak, and peering through the window she glimpses his helmet—"to which for crest the golden dragon clung of Britain," disappearing in the mist and gloom as he rides away "to slay and be slain."

And near him the sad nuns with each a light
Stood, and he gave them charge about the Queen
To guard and foster her forevermore.
And while he spake to these his helm was lowered,
To which the golden dragon clung
Of Britain; so she did not see his face
Which then was as an angel's, but she saw,
Wet with the mists and smitten by the lights,
The Dragon of the great Pendragonship
Blaze, making all the night a steam of fire.

Overtaken by remorse she weeps bitterly, "I thought I could not breathe in that fine air, that pure severity of perfect light; I yearned for warmth and color which I found in Lancelot."

"Ah my God," she prays, "what might I not have made of thy fair world, had I but loved thy highest creature here? It was my duty to have loved the highest; it surely was my profit had I known; it would have been my pleasure had I seen. We needs must love the highest when we see it. Not Lancelot, nor another.

Chapter VIII

THE PASSING OF ARTHUR

The tide of evil which had been slowly rising now engulfed King Arthur and his Table Round. The fellowship of knights was split in three parts, one part following the King, one part following Lancelot, and one following Sir Modred, who long had treacherously planned and fought with secret slander and malice to bring about the destruction of the King.

In the final battle King Arthur, knowing well whose spite has laid waste his fair Court, seeks out the traitor, Sir Modred, and deals him a death blow; yet Modred, in the intensity of his hatred, raises himself up in the very throes of death, and cleaves Arthur's helmet, so that the King sinks dying to the ground. Knowing that his death was near, the King took thought to return his sword, Excalibur, to the Lady who had given it to him: the faery Lady of the Lake. Calling to him Sir Bedivere, he gave him the sword and commanded that he take it to the mystic lake and throw it into the water, and then return and tell him what he had seen. Bedevere, however, could not bear the thought of destroying so beautiful a sword and one hallowed, moreover, by use of the Great King, so that he hid it among the grasses at the lake's edge and returned. When Arthur asked him what he had seen he could only reply that he heard nothing but the roaring of the wind and saw nothing but the lashing of the waves. Arthur therefore rebuked him for having failed to carry out his instructions and sent him back again; and again his heart failed him, and again he returned to say, as before, that he had seen and heard nothing but wind and wave. A third time, then, Arthur commanded that he throw the sword into the Lake and to fulfil this act of obedience on his honor as a knight; when seeing there was no alternative, Bedevere did as he was bid. Mustering up his courage he threw the great sword far out into the Lake, when an arm arose out of the water, taking the sword by its hilt, and holding it aloft and brandishing it thrice, so that it shone like a burning light, and disappeared.

When Bedevere returned to Arthur and told him what he had seen the King knew that at last his order had been obeyed, and he asked that they carry him down to the shores of the Lake. The faithful knights did this, and when they neared the shore, behold, a barge approached over the waters, and in it sat the Three Beautiful Queens, Faith, Hope and Love, who, when they saw the dying King, uttered a cry of sorrow that seemed to rise and echo amongst the very stars. And they cried: "Dear brother, you have tarried too long with thy wound." They bade him prepare for the homeward journey, back to the Fairy Isle of Avalon.

As the mystic ship disappeared from sight, amid the soft chanting of angelic voices, Arthur bade farewell to his last few faithful disciples, saying: "The old order passeth, making way for the new; and God fulfils Himself in many ways."

Thus Arthur passes over to be King in other realms. After the healing of his grievous wound he will return again.

Many great World Teachers have chosen Christmas, or the Winter Solstice season, as the time most propitious to begin their earth mission. It was in this same day season that Arthur passed away from the earth, in that ending of life which is its beginning in a higher world. As the poet sings of that fateful night, "It was the time when the light of heaven reached its lowest orb in the rolling year."

To the esotericist the passing of the Great King of the Grail cycles is more than the death of a military and secular leader, however, exalted, however noble and illumined. This passing marks the conclusion of a Mystery epoch.

Therefore the last battle in which King Arthur is slain is a type of the Biblical Armageddon, the end of an age. It is the battle of the True with the False:

> *Evolution ever climbing after some ideal good,*
> *And reversion ever dragging evolution in the mud.*

The Round Table was the "image of the mighty world," or archetypal pattern which God made and pronounced good. Twelve books recount its history. It lasted twelve years, and crashed with the exposure of the love of Lancelot and Guinevere. Arthur himself is the type of the Teacher for the Age in whom the Spirit of the Age dwells, who is forced by the failure of his disciples to withdraw from the earth and to await another cycle in the evolution of the world-soul to return and complete his work. To the Welsh Arthur stands for the star Arcturus in the constellation Bootes, which is called the Chariot of Arthur and is reminiscent of the Biblical Chariot of Elijah in which the prophet ascended living into heaven. "The seven clear stars of Arcturus" are "Arthur's Table Round," so called because they roll through such a round in the heavens, describing a circle around the Pole Star.

A Mystery Temple built on the earth plane usually continues its physical existence for about five hundred years. The School which is responsible for the Temple continues to work, but it may transfer its activities to another place where the evolutionary conditions are such as require its presence. The School at Glastonbury founded by Joseph of Arimathea was completing a five-hundred-year cycle at the time of the passing of Arthur. Tragic as it was, yet the karmic harvest must be reaped in its proper hour, and the seeds sown anew. The mystery of the relationship between the "White Abbey" (Glastonbury) and the Castle Carbonek has yet to be solved.

From five hundred A.D., which was the opening era of the Piscean Age, the focus of power shifted to the city of Rome and to the Bishop of Rome; as indeed we see in the story that among the hordes of European peoples who overran Rome after Constantine moved the capital of the Roman Empire to Constantinople, was this same King Arthur, who, according to the legend, was crowned Emperor in Rome itself by the Pope—not because he had repudiated the Holy School at Glastonbury but because he looked upon himself as Constantine's successor and was therefore crowned in the "State Church" of the Empire at Rome.

In these pages we have confined our attention to the purely esoteric interpretation of the legends, but we may observe in passing that the rise of the Church of Rome, and its Bishop usurping supreme power, is hinted in these legends as the real underlying cause of the loss of the Holy Grail.

In *The High History of the Holy Grail,* which dates to the thirteenth century, we read that after Percival had found the Castle of the Holy Grail and restored its wounded King to health, he sent the lesser hallows away to the hermits of the forest, who built holy churches and houses above them "in the lands and in the islands." But he himself took the Holy Grail to the city of Sarras. This can only mean that several Schools or Temples were built, not only at various places in the British Isles, but on the continent of Europe; and one of these is unquestionably that "House of the Holy Spirit" founded by him who was in a former life Lazarus, known to later history by the symbolical name of Christian Rose Cross who founded the Order of Rosicrucians.

Again in *The High History of the Holy Grail* we read: "The Grail appeared at the Sacring of the Mass, in *five several manners that none ought to tell . . . and King Arthur beheld the changes; the last thereof was the change into a chalice."* And the author adds that until this (Arthur's) time the chalice-type of Grail was not known anywhere. It is the chalice which we see in the Morte d' Arthur. The four Hallows represent the four elements: Fire, Air, Water and Earth—Spear, Cup, Sword and Dish—with a fifth signifying the Fiery Aether.

The School founded by Lazarus, however, is not the same as the Holy Grail of Glastonbury or the House of the Fisherman King in Rome. The Order of the Rose Cross includes all that has ever been known and taught in the mystic congregations, and is second to none in its reverence of Jesus of Nazareth; yet it has a tradition and a technique of its own as well and is not to be confused with the Mystery School of the Holy Grail as that was known in medieval Europe, through having all things in common with Joseph himself—for Lazarus was also a member of Joseph's party which brought the Grail to Europe.

Of this final stage of the Mystery School of the Holy Grail we shall learn in the Quest of Sir Galahad; and its correlation with the Order of the Rose Cross will be further shown in the discussion of Wagner's music-drama *Parsifal.*

PART IV

THE GALAHAD-PĀRSIFAL CYCLE

Chapter IX

THE CYCLE OF SIR GALAHAD

Ambassador of Spirit

Galahad came to Camelot at a time when the glory of King Arthur's Court was already drawing to a close. The youngest knight in the fellowship, for he was still a youth when knighted by the King, he was second to none in knightly prowess; even Sir Lancelot took no precedence over him either in feats of skill or strength.

Galahad, in the Vulgate, is the name of the great-grandson of Joseph, and is the same as Gilead, Numbers 26:29; Judges 10:18.

His lineage is obscure on his father's side; but through his mother he descends from "the first Bishop in Christendom," Joseph of Arimathea. A legend states that Galahad's father was "a fiend" who attacked a holy nun, that the infant of this union was taken by the convent and reared to young manhood until the time to send him to King Arthur's Court. Another legend has it that Sir Lancelot was his father and Elaine, daughter of King Pelles of the Castle Carbonek, was his mother, and that he showed the heredity from both, the knightly powers of his father and the saintliness of his mother. A third account identifies him with the Parsifal of German legend, or the Percival of the English cycle. Sir Arthur malory separates these accounts in his *Morte d' Arthur*, but it is possible to weave the Percival-Galahad cycles into one connected narrative; and while this lacks the studied and polished spirituality of the popular accounts, most notably that which Tennyson developed in *The Idyll of the King*, the esoteric significance emerges even more clearly.

However, the Galahad cycle as popularized by Tennyson and the Parsifal cycle as popularized by Wagner contain all of the essential esotericisms of the originals; and since these accounts are readily obtainable, we have chosen to follow them in the main features while adding such points from other sources as may throw added light upon the Grail Mysteries.

Those who are appointed "Ambassadors of Spirit" appear to have, even from infancy, some recognition of what their destiny is to be, and they begin early to prepare for this destiny, in childhood, almost as if with conscious deliberation.

The Abbey mural shows the infant Galahad clasping his hands together, gazing in rapt adoration at something invisible to those around him, while an expression of bliss overspreads his child's countenance. The nuns who have him in charge gaze upon him in awe, for they know that he sees what they cannot see, and hears what they cannot hear, of sights and sounds from angelic worlds. These nuns are no less than virgin servitors of the Grail attached to the Grail Castle Carbonek.

Galahad was still scarce more than a child—a youth of fifteen winters or thereabout—when he came to Arthur's Court. Such precocity is not unusual among old souls, for at this age, when other youths first feel the strong stirring of worldly ambitions and desires, the old soul experiences the remembered urge toward the things of Spirit. History affords many examples of this, from the boy Christ disputing in the Temple with the doctors to Joan of Arc leading her armies in battle.

There was great rejoicing throughout Camelot on the day that Galahad came to Arthur's Court. His coming was announced by marvels. On the river a red stone floated, in which by some miraculous means a sword was deeply thrust, and on its pommel were inscribed these words: "No man shall take me hence but he by whose side I should hang, and he shall be the best knight in the world." Seeing which, the King said to Lancelot, "Thou art the best knight, Lancelot," but Lancelot would not touch the sword, declaring that Merlin had prophesied that these marvels should come to pass in the day when the Sangreal was to be again manifest among men, and that whosoever touched the sword would suffer death by it, unless it were the knight to whom it rightfully belonged; and, he said, that knight was not himself.

Therefore the King and his knights returned to the great hall, and each knight sat down in his own place, and the banquet was begun with laughter and good fellowship, when of a sudden the doors and windows shut themselves, and the hall was in deep darkness, and no one in the hall dared move or make a sound. Then came a light which hovered over the Seige Perilous, where knight had never sat, and in the ghostly radiance each saw the face of his fellows looking one to another with awe and amaze.

And King Arthur arose from his seat at the high place of the circle and said: "Lords and fair knights, have no fear; we have seen strange things today, but stranger things are to come. Now I know that today we will see him who is to have the Seige Perilous and shall achieve the Holy Grail, which has been lost since Balin struck King Pelles; yet now it may be left to this noble Order to bring it to the land again. But only he may attain this Quest who hath clean hands and a pure heart, and valor and hardihood beyond other men."

He had not finished speaking before the outer door opened and there entered into the hall an old man robed all in white, with his head concealed, leading by the hand a youth clad all in red, wearing no armor, and carrying neither sword nor shield, though an empty scabbard hung at his side.

And the old man said to the King, "Lord, I bring thee this young knight who hath the blood of kings and is the kindred of Joseph of Arimathea; whereby the marvels of this court shall be fully accomplished."

It is an awe-inspiring moment, filled with reverence and exaltation. The other knights rise and with their sword make the sign of the cross, while an immense choir of adoring angels hover in the air above their heads. King Arthur arises from his throne to receive the new knight and gives him his blessing.

With our highest moments come also our greatest trials. Before Galahad stands the Seige Perilous, a chair carven with strange figures, and among them a scroll winding serpent-like with characters no man could read. This chair was formed through the magic of Merlin before he fell prey to the enchantment of Vivien. "Perilous for good or ill," Merlin had said, "for here no man could sit but he should lose himself."

Galahad, sustained by his spiritual preceptor, who corresponds to Gurnemanz* in the Parsifal epic, proclaims: "If I lose myself I

*Some interpretations say this Figure is Joseph of Arimathea, Galahad's ancestor.

save myself." The aged man puts upon Galahad a crimson robe trimmed with ermine and takes him by the hand and leads him to the Seige Perilous and lifts up the silken covering; and all behold and can now read the words inscribed there: "This is the seat of Sir Galahad, the good knight."

Sir Galahad sits in the Seige Perilous with the majesty of a Prince, and he dismisses the old man, asking that he commend him to "my grandsire King Pelles, and say that I will be with him soon." For Galahad knows that it is his destiny to heal King Pelles of the wound inflicted by Sir Balin, the savage young knight who stole the sacred Spear from the Castle Carbonek where these relics had long been guarded by the descendants of Joseph of Arimathea and King Evelake and their company.

We have seen that according to some accounts Lazarus, together with Martha and Mary, were of this saintly company which arrived in Britain and were given sanctuary by King Arviragus; and again, in later times, the name "Eleazar" occurs as the son of King Pelles. Now the name Eleazar is actually one spelling of the name given as Lazarus in the New Testament. We learn further that when Percival rode on his Quest, he was directed to "the Castle Goth" where he was told he would have news of Galahad, for there a cousin of Galahad's lived. In this we perhaps discover a hidden reference to the medieval castle, of Gothic design, in Germany, where "Lazarus," or Christian Rose Cross, founded the Order of the Rose Cross in the fourteenth century. The Eleazar of the Galahad story would be the brother of Galahad's mother.

In the matter of the Seats at the Round Table, as also of the Table of the Grail in a later place, the allegory reveals one of the deep secrets of the initiatory Schools.

There is, in every Mystery Temple on the inner planes, a "seat" or place reserved for each individual who belongs to that Temple; for this is a membership which goes back to the primeval sources of our solar system, when the life wave of human spirits, called virgin spirits, came forth fresh from the hand of God before they had run the cycle of involution. There are seven great "Rays" or streams of life, and each one is governed by a "Father Star." There are seven Mystery Schools in which the Nine Lesser Mysteries are given, and each school is governed by one of these seven Father Stars, and its members are all fellow-spirits who came forth from that Star in the beginning. Therefore each individual has a seat with his "name" written upon it in one particular Mystery Temple; but the Seige Perilous is the throne of the Master of the Temple.

After Galahad had been introduced to the Court, King Arthur took him down to the river and showed him the red stone floating with sword thrust deep therein, and Galahad withdrew the sword with ease and put it in the sheath that hung empty at his side, which it fitted perfectly. And he said: "This is the enchanted sword which was Sir Balin's wherewith he slew by mistake his Brother Balan, who also slew him at the same time; and through him came the dolorous wound to my grandsire King Pelles, which is not yet whole, nor shall be till I heal him."

In these cryptic utterances Galahad reveals his mission to heal the disunion between the outer, or exoteric and orthodox Church, and the inner, or esoteric, Mystery Temple. Already in this early day a growing materialism was causing the churches in the West to reject and to persecute the true esoteric Temple and its Teachings. It is significant that King Arthur and all his Court are perfectly well aware that the Castle of Carbonek is the stronghold where the Grail is to be found, if it is to be found at all; yet it is invisible to all eyes since the sin of Amfortas, or King Pelles. In the Galahad legend it is Sir Balin Le Savauge who inflicts the wound; and this knight, as well as his brother, is actually a knight of King Arthur's Court, so that "three counties" are disrupted by his crime. For when he has attacked King Pelles, lightning strikes the Castle of Carbonek, and the whole countryside is devastated by famine, plague and natural cataclysms. The two brothers, Sir Balin and Sir Balan, also suffer the karma of this condition when they meet in a battle, with visors down, and slay one another, discovering their identities only after each has dealt the other a mortal wound, and they die with arms twined remorsefully and lovingly about one another.

Occultists know that the life man lives reflects itself in nature. Violent passions react in destructive fires; unbridled emotions in floods; deceptions and double-dealing in blight and mildew of crops; anger, resentment, sarcasm in biting and stinging insects. Only man himself can create conditions favorable to a new heaven and a new earth, which must come from within before it is established firmly without. It is such interior soul conditions, reflected through King Arthur's Court, which bring about its dissolution.

As King Arthur and Galahad and the company of knights stood on the river bank, Galahad with the sword taken from the stone, a lady came riding on a white palfrey and said to the King that Nacien (Nathan) the Hermit had sent word to the King that on this day the Holy Grail should appear in his house, and then she returned whence she had come.

And the King said, "Now I know that the Quest of the Grail shall begin, and all ye will be scattered so that nevermore shall I see ye again as ye are now; let me then see a joust and tournament amongst ye for the last time."

The tournament was held in the meadows outside Camelot, with the Queen and the other ladies of the Court watching from a tower. In this tournament, Galahad had no shield and wore only light armor and a helmet, yet in a short time he outfought all but Sir Lancelot and Sir Percival, after which they all went to evensong in the great minster and then to supper in the great hall.

And as they sat at a table, there was heard a great thunder, and in a flash of light the Holy Grail entered the hall not borne by hands, but appearing steadfast in the beam of light, covered with white samite, and at its appearing each person in the hall was miraculously fed with that soul food which most he delighted to have, whatever it might be, and then the Grail, having traversed the hall, disappeared as it had come, with suddenness.

And at once, upon its disappearance, impetuously Gawain leaped to his feet and announced that he would go in Quest of the Grail, and the others eagerly followed him in their vows. Arthur, with tears in his eyes, spoke: "Sir Gawain, Sir Gawain, thou hast set me in great sorrow, for I fear me my true fellowship shall never meet together here again; and surely never Christian king had such a company of worthy knights around his table at one time."

This he said, knowing that it was only the Knight of spotless purity and valor who was destined for the Quest of the Grail and that only he who sat in the Siege Perilous could achieve it.

Such, then, were the marvels of Galahad's coming and the foolishness of Gawain whose example set the whole Court aflame and brought to an end the glory of the King.

* * * *

The Grail and the Quest Are One

Now let us examine what has been revealed in this account of the true nature of the Holy Grail and the meaning of its Quest.

Only one knight among them all is destined for success, and this is Sir Galahad. The King will not go forth upon the Quest, for he knows that his work lies near at hand, which God called him to do in the beginning, and this he will continue to do until the end.

The knights of his Court, however, show themselves wanting in a sense of responsibility; they are rash and unrealistic of outlook. It is a maxim of the initiatory Path that when the call to seek the Light comes to any person, it comes in just those conditions that are right for him, however burdensome they may seem to be. Is a man called who has wife and children to support? Is a wife called whose family makes demands upon her strength and time? Is the workman called whose hours are passed in hard manual labor? Or the craftsman, or the teacher, or the law-giver, or the soldier whose days are at the command of others? Whatever the condition may be, the aspirant will never find the Light by tearing himself away from his duties and responsibilities. When he is ready, the Light, the Grail, will find him wherever he is, and as it fed the knights at King Arthur's Court, so it will feed, with all that is necessary to the day and the way, every person who seeks it with dedicated heart and with a mind set firmly and one-pointedly in the direction of the lodestar of Truth.

But even the Predestined One, the Ambassador of Spirit, must first prove himself in the trials of daily living before the Grail will reveal itself to him.

The initiatory Path traverses both heights and depths. It is a way of light, yet it has its valleys of shadow, as it leads upward to the supernal peaks of cosmic illumination. In the life of the Great

Exemplar the glories of the Transfiguration were followed by Gethsemane and Golgotha, and these again by the Resurrection and Ascension. The height of spiritual ecstasy must always descend into the valley of the common and the restricted, in which the understanding gained in the high place is put to the test.

Reference has been made previously to the part played by women in the Grail legends. Each knight took oath that he would choose but one maiden and remain faithful to her throughout life. We have also shown that the feminine principle, when linked with the lower desire nature, is the cause of all failure, but when linked with Spirit leads to success in the Quest. The Will and Reason, masculine principles of the human spirit, must guide and direct; Imagination and Love, the feminine principles of God, the Shekinah, or Glory, are called the *Presence of God.*

The purity, moral strength and mental illumination of the young Galahad could only attract that which was as pure and beautiful as himself. He met and loved a maiden by name Blanchefleur, or White Flower, but he does not take her in marriage at this time.

Like Parsifal he proceeds to the Castle of the Grail, which is Carbonek, his grandsire's citadel, and sees the Grail Procession, but fails to ask the fated question. He has indeed arrived at his goal; he sees the Procession of the Mysteries which King Pelles, his son Eleazar and the Court are not able to see, and he is baffled to find that the spell which holds the castle and its inmates in thralldom remains unbroken.

He finds King Pelles worn by suffering, tossing uneasily upon a couch in a sort of waking sleep. Upon the entire court, its knights, ladies and priests, the same dream-like spell is evident. This dream-like state signifies the stupor of materialism into which all mankind has fallen through misuse of the Love Power which has meant the loss of the Holy Grail. Conservation of the life force is necessary to spiritual awakening, in which all evil and suffering vanishes like a dream of the night.

They all, both men and women, knights and priests, feel intuitively the blessed release which the pure good knight has power to bring to the Castle.

As Galahad stands beside the sleeping King, almost overcome at the thought of the work that lies before him, he sees the wonderful procession of the Grail passing nearby, which Pelles and his Court are now to chill and insensate to behold. "Only the pure in heart can see God." Only the pure can witness the visitation of angels who are so often with us as counsellors and inspiration.

> *Young men whom no one knows went in and out*
> *With a far look in their eternal eyes.*

Galahad sees the Angel of the Presence. He sees two knights, each with a seven-branched candlestick, another knight who holds aloft the bleeding spear and a maiden with a golden dish—the contrary symbol of Herodias, who carried the head of John the Baptist and used it for purposes of black magic. Here the Dish is sacred to the Christ. Power used either for good or evil is the same power, and power as such is not evil.

But like Parsifal, Galahad must return to the world, departing from the Castle of the Grail to perform some needed service, to amend some fault or shortcoming and so to gain the wisdom and compassion which will enable him to ask the fated question.

The mystic possesses faith; he knows intuitively what Truth and Goodness mean, but he does not possess understanding. It is the blending of two things—faith, or intuition, with understanding—that is Wisdom. It has been said that Wisdom is crystallized pain. This is virtually the universal experience, for men will learn no otherwise than through sorrow and suffering. Therefore the Way is long and hard, and for each one the achievement of the Quest is long deferred. Many lifetimes are spent in its pursuit. Through disappointment, heartache, disillusionment, the light may sometimes seem no more than a phantasm of the night, and only he who is persistent and patient will follow Galahad to the end of the Quest.

In Galahad's life the failure came when he did not marry Blanchefleur, who was his predestined wife, for in the Kingship of the Grail a certain maiden was sent to earth to rule with a certain King, and the King must marry and live a chaste life of Christian love, leaving a son to rule after him. This is not a dynasty of celibates, as in the Church.

Galahad's Girdle or Sword-Belt

Just before Galahad departed on his journey to the Castle of the Holy Grail, Percival's sister makes a belt for Galahad's sword with her own hands: "The wan sweet maiden clean from her forehead sheared away all that wealth of hair which made a silken network for her feet, and out of that she plaited, broad and long, a strong sword belt, and wove with silver thread and crimson in the belt a strange device, a crimson Grail within a silver beam." Binding the belt about Galahad she said:

> *My love, my knight of heaven, whose ideal*
> *Is one with mine, I bind thee with my belt.*
> *Go forth, for thou shalt see what I have seen*
> *And break through all till one shall crown thee King,*
> *Far in the Spiritual City.*

In esoteric symbology, the hair from which the maiden weaves the sword-belt represents the vital principle; hence its importance in all so-called magical rituals and practices of the black arts. The girdle signifies the protecting aura of the mind which is fixed on spiritual things: the engirdling "wedding garment" of the two higher ethers which enhalo the soulbody.

Galahad must therefore retrace his path, fulfill certain labors, come once more to Blanchefleur, and enter into marriage with her, after which he will complete the Holy Quest and accomplish his mission.

Galahad Returns to the World to Fulfill His Destiny

Having gone forth into the wilderness of the world once more, Galahad takes up those labors of the soul which every aspirant must perform on the way to the Grail and to the Spiritual City.

In the valley below Camelot, he came upon his first adventure, the encounter with the Loathly Damsel and her two companions. Here for the first time he learns why he failed at the Castle of the Grail. Bitterly the Damsel reveals to him his fault, and shows him that he should have made question of the conditions he found there.

The three maidens typify the three personality-principles of man: the physical, the etheric and the astral, or desire, body. It is Desire which is the dominant power of these three corporeal principles. All three are garbed in dark apparel. The second maiden carries a lash with which she drives forward the steeds of the other two. The Loathly Damsel was once a beautiful maiden, but now her countenance is distorted with evil passions. She is the counterpart of Kundry in Wagner's *Parsifal.*

Modern mental science is rediscovering the part which thought and emotion play in the health and beauty of the physical body. Envy, hatred, malice, every sort of evil emotion and every sort of evil thought leaves its mark in the organs of the body. The Loathly Maiden hurled fierce invective against Galahad, blaming him for her lowly and degraded condition. Galahad sorrowfully admitted that this was true, realizing, as every aspirant must in moments of self-revelation, that he is himself responsible for the loathsome images which drive through his imagination and emotions, at least in the passive sense of permitting them entry from without.

Later, when Galahad has attained the powers of the Holy Grail, the Loathly Damsel is made wholesome and beautiful again. Her transformation is symbolic of the awakening of the Divine within every human being, whose awakening causes him to manifest the beauty and wisdom which are his supernatural heritage.

Galahad's next adventure was to meet in mortal combat seven evil brothers, the seven deadly sins of the Christian neophyte. They are encased in dark grey armor, and they stand guard over a castle in which are imprisoned seven beautiful and holy maidens. Galahad met these seven brothers in combat one by one, and overcame them all.

The seven deadly sins are envy, sloth, lust, anger, gluttony, pride and avarice. Until the aspirant has made some progress toward eradicating these seven deadly sins, he cannot advance very far upon the Path of Attainment. The gray armor points to the grey and dark colors shown in the aura of the person who is still subject to these sins, for fear in one form or another attends upon them all, and grey in the aura is the significator of fear.

After Galahad's conquest of the seven brothers, an old man appeared who gave him a key to the castle wherewith to liberate the seven lovely maidens. This key is self-control. The old man is again the Wise Man, the Magus, Gurnemanz, who represents

Wisdom, the Wisdom which Galahad has won through the over-coming of the seven evil brothers, or sins, which then made it possible for him to acquire their corresponding virtues and powers.

There are seven important spiritual centers largely dormant within the auric envelope of every individual, which can be awakened only by means of spiritual development. These are the seven lovely maidens imprisoned in the castle by the dark brothers. So long as the aspirant is dominated by the seven sins, the powers lie dormant, sleeping, awaiting the coming of their emancipator. When Galahad enters the castle, the maidens, arrayed in beautiful colors, rush forward to greet him with great joy. These colors are again auric significators, a certain color characterizing each of the centers, which ray forth in the aura and produce magnificent spectacles visible to the clairvoyant. Clairvoyance, clairaudience, ability to function apart from the body at will, conscious Invisible Helper-ship and other spiritual powers ac-company the awakening of these vortices.

Liberating the souls in purgatory is not the work of Christ alone, nor yet of archpriests. Every Invisible Helper spends at least a portion of his time, when apart from the body, in exploring the purgatorial region and doing what he can to help the souls there, instructing them in the true nature of the spiritual worlds and aiding them to learn their lessons so that they can rise more speedily from their sorrows into the beauty and bliss of heaven.

The Maiden's Castle in the Inner World, the center of life; the outer world is the world of death. The dead are the truly living; those we call the living are in truth the dead. So long as the quest of *things* supersedes the quest of Spirit, so long as man lives in the separative consciousness of "me and mine" and devil take the hindmost, he is living in the death-consciousness and not in life. All are refreshed and encouraged by the coming of Galahad. This is the purpose of the life and work of one who is an Ambassador of Spirit.

Now at last Galahad returns to Blanchefleur, the White Flower, and marries her, and the next morning he sets out again for the Castle of the Holy Grail, completing the labors which it is his destiny to perform.

Galahad Leaves His Bride

This incident signifies the sacrifice of the personal life to the life of service, which is undoubtedly the most difficult initiatory test of all, but one that each must meet in some life upon the Way of true attainment.

The high and holy purpose of Galahad's marriage to Blanche-fleur leaves no room for personal sorrow, since in this union Galahad goes forward to complete the Quest with the masculine and feminine united within himself.

Arriving the second time at Carbonek, Galahad finds there Sir Percival and Sir Bors and nine other knights, three from Gaul, three from Ireland and three from Denmark. This time Galahad does not fail to ask the question which is to release the Castle from its spell.

King Pelles and his son are sent away, and when they have departed, Galahad sees four angels descend from heaven, carrying a chair in which is seated his ancester, Joseph of Arimathea, "the first Bishop of Christendom," whom the four angels set before the silver table on which the Grail stands. Then the door opens and again four angels enter, two bearing waxen candles, the third a towel and the fourth a bleeding spear which drips into a box which the angel holds in his other hand. The angels places the sacred objects on the table with the Grail, then Joseph takes the bread to serve Mass, and Galahad sees the image of a child smite itself into the bread, which Joseph puts into the Cup. And after the knights have given one another the kiss of peace, they are all fed from the Grail; but Joseph vanishes away. Even so is the Grail Feast served to every disciple on a silver platter just when the time is most opportune.

As the knights sat at the holy table in dread, they "saw a man come out of the holy vessel that had all the signs of the passion of Jesus Christ bleeding all openly, and said, "My knights and my servants and my true children, which be come out of deadly life into spiritual life, I will now no longer hide myself from you, but ye shall see now a part of my secrets and of my hidden things." The Christ then ministered to Galahad and the knights as he had ministered to the disciples at the Last Supper, after which He said that the land had grown evil and the Grail must be taken away to Sarras once more, to the spiritual place, and that Galahad must take it there. But first he is to "take of the blood of this spear for to anoint the mained king, both his legs and all his body, and he shall have his health."

What is the question which Galahad must ask? It concerns the mystery of the Sacred Four Letters, the Tetragrammaton, which stands in the place of the Ineffable Name of God. These four letters are the four cosmic roots of creation. They signify the four mystical elements, Fire, Earth, Air and Water, and their working for the union which produces the cosmos. St. John says that "the Word was made flesh" in Christ Jesus, and this is also implicit in the Grail story, for both in Malory's *Morte d' Arthur* and in the *High History of the Holy Grail* the Christ is seen to rise up out of the Cup which has been blessed by the mighty Hierophant Joseph of Arimathea. It is then *The Grail Himself* who sends Galahad and his two companions to Sarras, the Holy City.

When we turn to Wagner's *Parsifal* we find that Parsifal anticipates the true question when he asks, "WHO IS THE GRAIL?" and Gurnemanz replies:

> *That tell we not; but if thou hast of*
> *Him been bidden*
> *From thee the truth will not stay hidden.*
> *The land to Him no path leads through,*
> *And search but severs from Him wider*
> *When He Himself is not the guider.* *

The Mass of the Grail (Initiation) being done, Galahad takes the spear to heal King Pelles, and King Evelake, still living after three centuries, kisses his descendant and successor and ascends to heaven. Joseph of Arimathea is Galahad's teacher as well as his spiritual ancestor, for in all Mystery Schools the time comes when the Teacher calls his disciple "Son," even though there may be no blood relationship whatever. The veil which has hidden the

---

*The Metropolitan Opera libretto uses the word "It" instead of "Him" in these verses. The lines quoted here are from Max Heindel's "Mysteries of the Great Operas."

mysteries of life is the same as the Veil of Isis, whose mysteries are always hidden from the profane and revealed to the pure in heart.

Life and light now break forth from the Grail, awakening and vitalizing all who dwell within the Castle and the Court. The King, priests, knights and ladies are nourished with the wondrous substance of the Grail and made whole; which means that the earth and its humanity are regenerated and redeemed through pure and holy living and the building of the power of the Holy Grail within—a power which is the true atomic force.

Galahad bends in affection above the dying King; the eyes of King Pelles are lifted to behold the Grail, and seeing, he receives blessed comfort and release from pain and suffering.

King Pelles (or Amfortas) signifies our present earth humanity, which lives amid suffering and limitations caused by the misuse of the sacred life forces. Galahad represents the pioneers of the new race, living and teaching the way to regeneration through purity.

The three Knights from Arthur's Court are instructed to take the Grail and Spear to Sarras, for a ship awaits them in the harbor below the Castle. As they ride forth the countryside is smiling and serene, crops flourish, men and women are happy and smiling; for the curse has departed from the land.

The knights are taken in a small boat to the ship, on whose sails they see the sign of the Red Cross, and in the ship awaiting them is the silver table, and on the table the Grail covered with red samite; and a great and splendid bed on which Galahad should sleep, called Solomon's Bed. For this was the ship called Solomon's Ship, of which many wondrous things were told.

When Solomon built this ship he foretold that it was to be used by one of his line, a man who should be also a maid, and that it should bear him to the holy city of Sarras. In the wonderful vessel Solomon placed a bed with a crown upon it, and at its foot the sword of David of the line of Judah. The bed was enclosed by a frame composed of two rods rising perpendicularly from the center of each side and crossed by a third above. These *three rods* are of three symbolic colors, white for chastity, green for compassion and long suffering, and red for charity. They come from the Tree of Life and have undergone three changes in color corresponding to the primeval innocence, the fall, and the redemption. In the *three rods* we have a reference to the right-angled triangle which was an important measuring device to ancient builders and which remains symbolic of the builder's mysteries in Masonry today. It is the Pythagorean Triangle of the Greek Mysteries and possesses profound philosophical meanings far beyond the mere mathematical usage.

Solomon's Ship means divine Wisdom through which the soul body is built. That it is Solomon's Ship in which Galahad is to sail reveals a mystery: namely, that Solomon was the founder of the kabbalistic School which is figured in the Grail. Solomon's name means "Wisdom of the Sun." The Ship's colors were also Galahad's colors, white for stainless purity, green for compassion and long suffering, red for the love power and light of the Holy Spirit which went ever with him.

In all Grail legends the inner meaning parallels the outer, so that each meaning may be read separately or together with the other; and while the outer legend is poetic and touches the heart, the inner is a discipline for the mind and spirit. Thus in all esotericism spiritual teachers use the symbolism of the ship to indicate the "soul body" or "celestial body," as Paul describes it, in which the illumined one rises into the angelic realms. For among esotericists it is well known that the soul is not a mere cloud or formless gust of wind, but that the human ego, wherever it may be, tends to put forth some sort of embodiment as a plant puts forth blossoms, and this phychical body "sails," as it were,, in an aura of light. Hence in Scriptures and Apocrypha "boats" and "ships" point to events which happen in the soul world, either when the "terrestrial" (physical) body is asleep or when the ego has withdrawn from it into its "psychical" or celestial body in some initiatory rite, sailing aloft in its auric vessel.

The new Christed Initiation, which was just received by Lazarus, differed from the ancient form in that due to a higher stage of unfoldment the former trance conditions was no longer necessary for the new Christed Initiation. The Initiation belonging to the new Christed Dispensation is received in full waking consciousness, using neither hypnosis nor drugs.

The Initiation of Lazarus was therefore not the trance state of antiquity but the conquest of death itself and the inauguration upon earth of a new initiatory method.

The "New Jerusalem," or City of the Holy Grail, is not the mere physical city of wood and stone. It is a Mystery Temple located in the etheric realms high over its physical counterpart, which in its present condition is truly a distorted shadow of the spiritual archetype which glitters above it like a crown (or "island"). Here to this day the Lord Christ, the blessed Mary, the disciples and the holy men and women who created the early Christian community continue to meet and work with those yet living on earth, if they are sufficiently advanced to come to them there.

Many beautiful stories of the early Christian Church show with what eagerness the "followers of the Way" looked to each Sun's Day, which they adopted instead of Saturn's day of the Old Dispensation. Some indeed could visit the initiatory halls in full waking consciousness; others remembered as a dream what there they had known and seen. Still others brought back only a sense of radiant happiness, with no clear memory of its source, though they divined its cause. St. John's experience in this Holy City he has incorporated in the Book of Revelation, which, though it is an allegory, is more than allegory in that it conveys under poetic similitudes a hint of conditions that have real existence in the soul world.

When Galahad entered the holy place he was received with great rejoicing. The Master truly stated when He was with men on earth that there is more rejoicing over one lamb that has been found than over the ninety-nine safe in the fold. So also there is great joy among the Emancipated Ones when one who still lives in the dark body of earth learns to sever the bonds and soars, freed from his chains, to work at will in the cosmic fields of the higher realms. It is here that Galahad comes to stand before the Tree of Life laden with golden fruits, which are the rewards of transmutation of the seven deadly sins into powers of the spirit: Faith, Hope, Love, Compassion, Service and Universality.

Galahad now joins those Emancipated Ones whom St. John

describes in Revelation as standing upon the Sea of Glass and bearing the Name of the Lamb on their foreheads. He has claimed for his own the most glorious heritage which man, while living upon this earth, can ever know: the first-hand experience of *conscious immortality;* for, as the poet sings, he has found "a life beyond this life."

St. John states that the leaves of the Tree of Life, which are green and signify the knowledge of inner plane mysteries, are for the healing of the nations. Such is the exalted state achieved by Sir Galahad, who is the perfect type pattern of the Christed man of the New Age, in whom we see as in a glass the image of what the New Age man shall be in the plenitude of his powers. This is not something limited to the members of a single cult or sect; it is the promised pattern for the entire human race. Here Sir Galahad is, in himself, the symbol of the 144,000 "saved"—a kabbalistic cipher signifying all mankind as Adam's seed.

In these turbulent days filled with fear, suspicion, wars and rumors of wars, it is well that as modern aspirants upon the Way we lift minds and hearts in daily prayer, contemplating the fair bright day which awaits all humankind.

Chapter X

RICHARD WAGNER AND
HIS MUSIC-DRAMA PARSIFAL

Wagner: Philosopher—Mystic—Musician

The nineteenth century in Europe was a philosophical age, in which many of the great creative minds turned to the ancient world for the great mystic truths which, immortal in the human soul, are continually re-embodied in works of art. Such a mind was Richard Wagner, who loved philosophy with the deep ardor of the mystic, and who sought to show it forth among men in an art form supremely beautiful. He has left many records which show the unfolding of the Mystery Wisdom in his heart and mind; but even without his own written testimony, his music-dramas tell the story in language which cannot be misunderstood by any one who know the basic principles involved.

It was his dream that every performance of *Parsifal*, which was the culminating work of his life and the supreme love of his heart, should be, as it were, an initiatory experience to all who witnessed it; and for this reason he said that it should never be produced outside of Beyreuth, where it could be suitably housed and shown, ensphered in an atmosphere of profound reverence and wonder. Despite his command, *Parsifal* has been shown in many places in the world since his passing; and while there can be no question but that something is lost to these performances which only Beyreuth can give, still its wondrous mysteries penetrate to the core of every heart and awaken there the holy living ardor of the Grail Itself, with deepening concepts of self-dedication to the higher life.

The writer once spent four years in New York City and one of the high spiritual lights of each one of these four years was the Good Friday performance of *Parsifal* at the Metropolitan Opera House.

Wagner's *Parsifal* tells the story of the Grail hero of Chretien de Troyes and Wolfram von Eschenbach, and although these two ancient troubadours were not at one in their views on the Holy

111

Grail, yet they are the unquestioned authorities to whom all later writers have turned for instruction and illumination. Wagner wrote the libretto for Parsifal in 1871, two years after Tennyson had retold the story of Galahad at length in English in his *Idylls of the King*. The music was composed in 1878, and 1879, and the opera was first performed at Beyreuth in 1882, with Wagner himself on the conductor's stand. We may comment in passing that these librettos which Wagner wrote stand preeminent in German poetry; and even if he had not become more famous as the composer of operas, his fame as a poet would still have been assured from the poetry he wrote for those operas.

We have said before, many times, in writing of Wagner's operas*, that Wagner's music in the Grail epics, *Lohengrin* and *Parsifal* are transcriptions of angelic melodies such as the mystic hears with spiritual hearing; and concerning which Burne-Jones, the English artist who painted many pictures of Grail subjects, wrote in 1884: "I heard Wagner's Parsifal the other day. . .He made sounds that are really and truly (I assure you, and I ought to know) the very sounds that were to be heard in the San Graal chapel."

Richard Wagner's music has gained world-wide popularity since those first momentous years when it was attacked on every side; but even today, there are comparatively few who fully appreciate or comprehend the exalted spiritual truths which he has hidden within the dramatic situations and given sound to in the music patterns. This is pure New Age music. When Initiation is again the center of all spiritual work, and when Wagner's music has come into its own, it will be part of the initiatory work of the New Day.

In accultism it is known that there are seven major centers in the body, and many other centers attendant upon these, which are responsive to musical vibrations. In ancient times, the sacred chants played upon these force centers—the music of masses and chorales served to stir them from their sleep—but in modern times there are many who could no longer respond to the ancient

RICHARD WAGNER AND THE MUSIC-DRAMA PARSIFAL   113

modes. Something new was required to vibrate with the soul of the epoch, and this Wagner's music has provided.

Each one of the characters in the music drama is symbolic of a state or stage of spiritual unfoldment in the individual; representing definite qualities or powers. This is described in the musical motif which always attends the appearance of this character on stage, and which may also speak of him in his absence. To the spiritual vision this motif is an aura of light and color which surrounds the character it represents.

The first of the major centers to be awakened, after the aspirant has lived the life of purity and harmlessness for a suitable period of time, is the chakra, or blossom, at the root of the spine, where the spirit-fire sleeps. The awakening of this fire and its ascent up the spine toward the organs in the head results in the stimulation of the other six centers, which are also largely dormant. Hence ancient teachers often referred to the spinal canal as "the Path of Initiation."

Parsifal is the type of aspirant who has gone far on the Path in former incarnations and is now ready to ascend the high passes of the Mount of the Holy Grail, becoming the Initiate.

The Parsifal motif plays directly upon the several chakras or force centers of the etheric body, vibrating each one singly and together, in harmonious spiritual unfoldment. Parsifal's Initiation, however, since it applies to the modern world, shows variations from that of the ancients.

The solar plexus was the center most commonly awakened through the pre-Christian Initiation. Since it is the center of life forces which can be used for evil as well as for good, it, like the lowest or sacral center, had to be "conquered" and brought under the control of the will. The solar plexus could become the gateway for the lowest and most sinister forms of psychism if the will were not firmly pointed toward the Most High. Upon this center plays the motif of Amfortas, who was originally a noble aspirant but one who lost his high place through the seduction of the beautiful maiden Kundry. However, before his death he becomes regenerated through the powers of the Holy Grail and the Holy Spear which Parsifal wields.

The force center in the spleen is the source of the renewal of vitality. When it is fully awake and under the control of the illumined will, man is able to flood his entire body with the life forces which pour in from the sun and from outer space. Eventually, old age and even death itself will be no more. It is the motif descriptive of the holy Titurel which impinges upon the force center of the spleen. Titurel was formerly the head of the Grail Castle and teacher of its Knights, until he relinquished his power to his son, Amfortas. This holy man had bridged the chasm between waking and sleeping, between life and death. He was in full possession of his faculties both night and day, and also between death and rebirth. Since Amfortas had failed in his guardianship of the Grail, Titurel remained in the background of the work until Amfortas' successor should come. By means of first-hand experience he had come into the knowledge that all life is continuous and all life is one.

The heart center is connected with the most exalted phases of transmutation. Its musical motif is that of Kundry, who is the symbol of transmutation in the Parsifal legends. She tempts the knights, and if they fall prey to her temptations, they are lost to the Path. But if, like Parsifal, they stand firm, then she becomes the servitor of the Initiate, leading him to the Castle of Light, where she dies on the steps of the altar, her sacrifice made perfect in the perfect knight whom she has served, who stands illumined and transformed by the powers of the Grail.

The white and glittering beauty of the Lance motif plays upon the force center in the throat. The Lance motif symbolizes the power of Truth in manifestation, and it is truth that always manifests in the power of the Creative Word.

The motifs of the Eucharist and Grail are direct transcriptions of pure angelic music, and they play immediately upon the pituitary and pineal glands respectively, which are located in the head.

To the clairvoyant vision, the spinal spirit-fire, as it is awakened at the base of the spine and ascends through the spinal canal, forms as it were the likeness of the stem of a flower, its light reaching forth in petals of radiant color to the organs of the physical body which are the foci of their powers. Thus the base of each lily-like flower intersects the spine, and as the blossom continues to unfold, its light reaches to the uttermost limits of the aura; then farther and farther, until in the Transcendent Master they are lost in the depths of spiritual space.

There is an etheric organ, little mentioned in occult literature, which is built from the life substance as it rises from the throat center up into the head. It has the shape of a lily-cup, whose corolla shines within the skull, embracing the organs of spiritual vision which are there and sending its light outward to radiate halo-like about the head. This etheric structure is a true organ, though it has as yet no physical counterpart, and it is the destined instrument which will enable perfected man to speak the Creative Word, whose sound verily has the power to create and recreate matter in all its forms.

The Mystery of the Grail is the Mystery of Sound and Light. Parsifal learned to use these powers rightly, but only after suffering and sorrow. He *asked the right question*, the why and wherefore of evil and suffering on earth (Why does Amfortas suffer?), and in learning the answer to this question he became the King of the Holy Grail, joined with Christ in the work of salvation. He knows *who* and *what* the Grail is.

In orthodox theology that aspect of Godhead which imparts celestial virtues or graces to the human soul is called the Holy Ghost or Holy Spirit, and for this reason medieval poets have called the Castle of the Grail "the House of the Holy Spirit."

Thus the old legend shows that the New Age man figured in Parsifal will build the Grail Cup within himself and that the Castle which houses it is the body, which is indeed the Temple of the Grail and House of the Holy Spirit.

The Mystic Love Feast

The Holy Grail and the Mystic Love Feast (the Eucharist) are inseparable. There can be no Love Feast without the Grail. The Love Feast has been the nucleus of Temple Mysteries since the beginning of time, and this is the theme of the immortal Grail and Eucharist motif in *Parsifal*.

In the Temple scene the Grail is exposed, the Knights kneel in prayer. Suddenly the Grail glows with rubescent life, and angels sing in ecstasy. What has happened? It is the spiritual force which the knights have generated within themselves by means of prayer that goes forth to bless the world and which causes the Cup to glow. This power is the same as that which the early Christian Initiates poured into the Bread and Wine of the Mystic Repast, and which became the medicine of health and wholeness to all who suffered. Today in all genuine Mystery Schools a like Mystic Supper is celebrated at about the hour of sundown, and in the Temples at midnight. The prayers which are poured forth to a center are gathered up and sent out to the world for help and healing. The "charged Bread and Wine" are today as of yore the Panacea or Elixer sought by the spiritual alchemist.

Those who are able to do this work are the most exalted of human souls. It is for those of the innermost circle. In the Chemical Marriage of Christian Rosenkreuz we are shown a chamber in which a globe hangs centrally, and upon this globe beats the light from suns which shine upon it from every side. What are these suns but the radiant auras of the presiding Initiates, who are thus bringing to a focus on the globe the high powers of Him who is the Grail? And what is that globe but the earth itself?

The Sacred Spear and the Grail figure in the Mystic Repast together, as they were together on Golgotha. Before Parsifal can heal Amfortas, the point of the Spear must glow as the Cup glows. The Spear represents the spinal spirit fire which, when lifted to the head, touched with fire the pineal gland and pituitary body. In the lily cup which then shines forth, the Essence, the Panacea, is found, which heals the world and all the ills of mankind. This is the key to all so-called "magnetic" healing and all healing by prayer.

The evil Klingsor could not use the Sacred Spear; he had not its power. But in the hands of Parsifal it could dissolve the evil garden created by Klingsor's dark magic.

Melchizedek, the title of a succession of Atlantean High Priests, gave this secret of high magic to Abraham, as shown in the Old Testament, where he celebrated with Abraham the Mystic Supper in which also he conferred upon Abraham the High Priesthood of the then New Dispensation of the Aryan Epoch and Aryan Age.

Christ Jesus, the supreme World Teacher, transmitted the Teaching to His disciples as the culmination of His earthly mission. Its true meaning has been all but forgotten, but in the Aquarian Age it will be revived in all its mystic potency.

Only "the Few" now comprehend its deep inner import. Yet with or without knowledge, no observance of the Eucharist in Christ's Name is ever unattended by a tremendous downpouring of the angelic power, and always there is the angelic choir chanting, "Love grows cold without the observance of the Mystic Love Feast."

PART V

CONCLUSION

Chapter XI

THE MODERN GRAIL KNIGHT AND HIS QUEST

There are aspirants in the world today who possess all the eager enthusiasm and high idealism of the knights of the Middle Ages.

Wherever in the world—regardless of race, color, creed or caste—there is anyone, whether alone or with a group, working earnestly, with deep spiritual intent, for world betterment and the uplifting of any of God's creatures upon this planet, there the Grail descends, bestowing gifts of power and illumination.

Wherever there is an occult or mystical group who are honest and sincere, who are working not to amass earthly treasure or to build up a powerful organization but to achieve the greatest good for the greatest number, to bring about the universal under-standing that all men are brothers because they are children of the same Father-Mother God, there the Grail descends, and its nearness is known in ever-increasing measure in the benediction of love, peace and beauty, wisdom and strength.

Many truth groups are founded in enthusiasm and flourish vigorously for a time, then are seen slowly to disintegrate, until they disappear altogether. Observing this, the casual onlooker comments, "How much time and effort have been wasted there!" This, however, is a superficial point of view. Always from such a disintegrated group will come forth a few—the remnant as it were—who have caught the vision and who go forth holding aloft the torch of light.

The majority of the knights who came to King Arthur's Court were unable to abide in the high vision of the Table Round. Yet out of their midst came Sir Galahad, who figures the few who are able to tread the Path victoriously to the very end, and thence to pass beyond through the portals of light.

It is well in this day of strife and tumult, of hatred and fear, to lift mind and heart frequently in contemplation of the noble young knight whose exalted vision and perfect attainment stand unchallenged, an inspiration to all who have taken up the Quest after him.

The word Initiation comes from a Greek word meaning "to enter into," and in the early Christian community was a term applied to the Baptism. In our own day Initiation is still truly an entering into a new life, a higher phase of consciousness in which we know Christ face to face and discover that we, like Him, are children of the Most High. Initiation is a shortcut to wisdom. To follow its strait and narrow up-ward-climbing Path is hard but enables one to accomplish in a few short lifetimes on earth what the masses of mankind will achieve only after many millenia. They are ascending, too, for God watches over His children wherever they may be, but they climb by slow and easy stages, on a broad road that winds gently around the mountain; whereas the initiated one, who is a Child of the Light, takes the rugged path upward which, though it cannot be said to shorten labor, since the actual labor of millenia is concentrated in a few lifetimes, yet brings him to the summit ages in advance of his brethren.

No one is ever forced to enter upon the steep Path which climbs dangerously to the summit. Each man must enter of his own free choice, but before he enters thereon there are certain preparations to be made, as always before an arduous undertaking, and the Guardians of the Way see that he is put to the test before essaying the Path. The requisite qualities are courage, devotion, persistence, discrimination and continuity of purpose. Some degree of these qualities must be present at the outset before leaving the broad highway of mass evolution, if Initiation is to be achieved. There are many who climb mountains; only a few conquer Mt. Everest.

In our discussions of the Holy Grail and the knightly epics of Initiation, we have drawn largely from Tennyson's *Idylls of the King*, because Tennyson has chosen, out of the great, bewildering mass of legends, those which best lend themselves to a philosophical and mystical interpretation. But in order to make clearer certain esoteric principles we have also drawn upon Malory's *Morte d' Arthur* and the anonymous *High History of the Holy Grail*, which is earlier. Thus we have elucidated some of the experiences which the aspirant today, as centuries ago, star the Path of the disciple, and we have shown how these experiences are a reflection of traits of character and understanding—or lack of them.

The Cycle

> of Pelleas and Ettarre—the proof that sorrow is ofttimes the great transformer.

The Cycle

> of Geraint and Enid—some of the processes which unfold in the course of the work of transmutation.

The Cycle

> of Merlin and Vivien—demonstrating the tragic mistake of following the mental path to the exclusion of the way of love and devotion, and thus failing to develop the equilibrium between head and heart, which is only achieved by giving one's self in loving, self-forgetting service.

The Cycle

> of Gareth and Lynette, in which is shown the great overcoming.

The Cycle

> of Elaine, Lancelot and Guinevere: "the mills of the gods grind slowly but they grind exceedingly small."

The Cycle

> of Galahad: "many are called but few chosen." Initiation was first given to mankind in the earliest dawn of civilization on this planet so that we might, if we so desire, forge ahead and carve out our destiny in advance of the masses.

This Path of the Higher Life was always and everywhere known in the pre-Christian world as the Path of Initiation. The early Christians called it The Way. For the medieval knight it was the Quest of the Holy Grail, and for the modern aspirant it is the Way of Attainment. The Path is the same and the Goal is One.

King Arthur's Round Table continued the School of early Christian Mysteries upon which all five of the Patriarchates of the World Church were founded, and it is these sacred Mysteries which form the Way of Attainment for the modern Grail knight as well.

When the Lord Christ departed from the earth He left the Cup of Remembrance to bring together all those who belonged to Him; and so it is said that from the early years of the Church, through the Orders of Chivalry and Mystery Schools such as King Arthur's Round Table, through Masonic and Rosicrucian brotherhoods and collegia, and down to the seekers of our own time, there is a golden chain, each link of which is a soul, binding all ages together in unity of Truth about the feet of the Christ.

Afterword

A critical evaluation of these great Grail classics is not the primary aim of our studies in the foregoing pages. Not alone through the medium of books are their inner meanings revealed. Let the aspirant go within and in so doing lay hold of the high visions the Grail legends inspire. Only so may they become the master key yielding access to a life beyond a life. For it is true of every man as it is of King Arthur: From the great deep he comes; to the great deep he goes.

APPENDIX I

The Cross and Grail

Plato said, "The world soul is crucified."

The horizontal limb of the cross represents the lines of force of certain archangelic beings, called Group Spirits, which circle the earth and impinge upon the horizontal spine of animals and the lateral branches of fruit trees.

The plants are represented by the lower limb of the cross. The Group Spirits of the plant kingdom function below the surface of the earth, sending their life forces upward into trees and plants.

Man is represented by the upper limb of the cross, and receives his spiritual sustenance from the sun through the head. In nature the open flower is the Grail Cup and the sacred spear is the sunbeam that opens the flower and represents the spiritual power that has been turned to so much destructiveness by the human race, but which will bring the resurrection when it is rightly used to help and heal.

As the flower draws the spiritual force or power from the sunbeam in a pure and chaste manner, and it unfolds in harmonious beauty, so the disciple must, through purity, chastity and compassion, develop the Grail Cup within his own body, the spiritualized Will Force acting as the positive agent of this work.

Let the aspirant visualize the White Rose in the center of the cross where the Christ Force centers at each of the four Seasons. This is the Cosmic Grail Cup. The life of the Christ correlates with the four turning points of the sun's annual cycle: Birth, Crucifixion, Resurrection and Ascension. To the opened eye of the mystic, there is a descent of power at the Autumn Equinox, which reaches the center of the earth at the Winter Solstice and then arises at the Vernal Equinox and is again enthroned in the Sun at the Summer Solstice.

APPENDIX II

IDYLLS OF THE KING

Correlated with the Months of the Year: a Mystic Calendar

1. Sun in Capricorn. Arthur's Birth.
2. Sun in Aquarius. Galahad, the Winged Man of the Future.
3. Sun in Pisces. Gareth and Lynette: Daffodils or Lenten lilies in bloom.
4. Sun in Aries. Castle built for Arthur at Camelot: Merlin Architect and Builder. Spiritual New Year.
5. Sun in Taurus. Marriage of Arthur and Guinevere: May.
6. Sun in Gemini. Geraint and Enid; Sir Balin and Sir Balan.
7. Sun in Cancer. Summer Solstice. Pentecost. Birth of Galahad.
8. Sun in Leo. Elaine and Lancelot. Full summer. "Orient windows open wide for heat."
9. Sun in Virgo. Pelleas and Ettare. Foreshadowing of fall: Late summer roses.
10. Sun in Libra. Vivien and Merlin. Descent of Darkness. Autumn Equinox.
11. Sun in Scorpio. Last Tournament. Early winter weather.
12. Sun in Sagittarius. Mist and Rain. Farewell to Guinevere.
13. Return of the Cycle: Sun in Capricorn; the end of all:
    > "deep midwinter in the frozen hills
    > that day when the pure light of heaven burned
    > at his lowest in the rolling year."

Arthur's twelve knights are, cosmically interpreted, the twelve signs of the zodiac. Arthur himself is the sun, or the Christ Light to be awakened in man, so that each man is the image of his spiritual king. The twelve Idylls are opportunities given for soul growth as the sun passes in its yearly cycle through the twelve signs.

APPENDIX III

SARRAS, THE SPIRITUAL CITY

Historians of the Grail are not agreed as to the geographical significance of the Spiritual City of Sarras. The name is associated in legend with "the confines of Egypt," "beyond Babylon" (like the Holy City seen in vision by Esdras in the Field of Ardath), "an island," the "New, or Heavenly Jerusalem" and "Syria" generally. We have chosen the meaning as "the heavenly Jerusalem" which is an "island" floating above the terrestrial city. Paradise is frequently described as such an island, floating cloud-like above the earth, in ancient cosmologies. Modern esotericists know that every city on earth has its heavenly prototype, which insofar as it pertains to the future, seems to float above the earthly city. Yet occasions are known of visionaries who are transported in consciousness into the "heavenly city" while still in the body of flesh, and it then seemed to them that the two were the same, though occupying different strata of consciousness.

That there are Egyptian overtones to Grail history is well known, since according to Von Eschenbach the story of the Grail was first written in Alexandria, in an early time, by one Flegetanis, whose mother was a descendant of Solomon and his father a "pagan" (Egyptian or Arab).

Von Eschenbach says that his account comes from Kyot de Provence who discovered the Grail story in a library at Toledo, and since it was written in Arabic, Kyot had to learn that language in order to decipher and translate it. In Toledo also rested the "emerald table," supposedly Solomon's, and one of the Cups supposed to be the Cup of the Last Supper. It is probable that the emerald table was an astronomical mosaic—it may have been a golden table inset with emeralds—for Toledo was the Greenwich of the medieval astronomer. Kyot de Provence seems to imply that the Grail story is written in the stars, and this many Christians still believe to be true.

APPENDIX IV

THE GLASTONBURY THORN

Anciently a center of Druid worship, Glastonbury survived the conquest of England, linking together the early and late Christianity of the island. Glastonbury Abbey is said by some to have been founded in the second or third century, which to some extent substantiates the claim of those who say that the original Grail Castle and dynasty were not located at Glastonbury, but elsewhere. Glastonbury flourished without interruption until Henry VIII hanged the last abbot, and the famous Abbey was allowed to fall into ruin. Henry's purpose in thus destroying Glastonbury may be guessed from the fact that he also put to death the last of England's archdruids.

At Glastonbury the Blood Spring (Chalice Well) marks the spot where according to one story the Grail was buried, or according to another, dropped into the well.

The famous Glastonbury Thorn, said to have been Joseph's staff, which he planted in the earth at Glastonbury where it took root and grew, blossoming forever after on Holy Night, was cut down by the Puritans in the seventeenth century; but offshoots of the original tree still grow there, beside the Blood Spring.